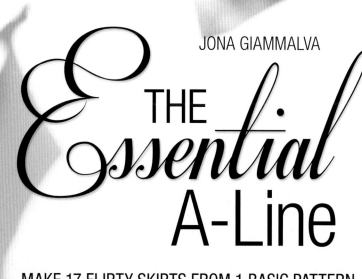

JONA GIAMMALVA

THE *Essential* A-Line

MAKE 17 FLIRTY SKIRTS FROM 1 BASIC PATTERN

SIZES 0 TO 20

D0557613

stashBOOKS®

an imprint of C&T Publishing

PUBLISHER | Amy Marson

CREATIVE DIRECTOR | Gailen Runge

ART DIRECTOR / BOOK DESIGNER |
Kristy Zacharias

EDITOR | Deb Rowden

TECHNICAL EDITORS | Alison M. Schmidt
and Gailen Runge

PAGE LAYOUT ARTIST | Kerry Graham

PRODUCTION COORDINATOR | Jenny Davis

PRODUCTION EDITORS | S. Michele Fry
and Joanna Burgarino

ILLUSTRATOR | Mary Flynn

PHOTO ASSISTANT | Mary Peyton Peppo

COVER IMAGE AND STYLE PHOTOGRAPHY
by Tea Ho

PHOTOGRAPHY by Diane Pedersen of
C&T Publishing, Inc., unless otherwise noted

Published by Stash Books, an imprint of C&T Publishing, Inc., P.O. Box 1456, Lafayette, CA 94549

Library of Congress Cataloging-in-Publication Data

Giammalva, Jona, 1965-

The essential A-line : make 17 flirty skirts from 1 basic pattern / Jona Giammalva.

   pages cm

ISBN 978-1-60705-669-0 (soft cover)

1. Skirts. I. Title.

TT540.G53 2013

646.4'37--dc23

                    2012031514

Printed in China

10 9 8 7 6 5 4 3 2 1

ACKNOWLEDGMENTS

This book could not have been written without the support and patience of my family. I want to thank my husband, Joey; my daughters, Olivia, Pietra, and Sofia; and my sons, Asher and Levi, for encouraging me, inspiring me, and eating lots of peanut butter and jelly sandwiches while I was busy sewing and writing.

I want to thank my parents, John and Ardie Ford, for giving me a colorful childhood and thinking everything I do is amazing.

A huge thanks to so many of my creative friends who bring much love and color to my life: Isaac and Heather Bailey, Bari Ackerman, Jamie Harned, Monica Solorio-Snow, Paula Prass, Kay Whitt, Mary Abreu, and Sandra Shanafelt.

Thank you, Susanne Woods, for thinking I could write a book before the thought had ever occurred to me.

Many of the fabrics and sewing supplies were provided by the wonderful folks at these companies: Michael Miller Fabrics LLC, Andover Fabrics, Dharma Trading Company, Coats & Clark, C&T Publishing, and Thomas Knauer.

I'd like to extend my gratitude to the wonderful designers whose fabrics are featured in a majority of the skirts in this book: Heather Bailey, Bari J. Ackerman, Amy Butler, Anna Maria Horner, Laura Gunn, Carol Van Zandt, Denyse Schmidt, Vicki Payne, and Violet Craft.

I want to also express my gratitude to all my blog readers. Over the years I have been blessed, inspired, and improved by the cheer, enthusiasm, and friendship they have given me. Thank you.

FOREWORD BY HEATHER BAILEY

I first met Jona when she helped out at a big magazine shoot for my Freshcut fabric collection. She and her daughters wrangled baby chickens, strung beads on party decor, and lugged props back and forth to our cars. That day, I was impressed with her easygoing, friendly, and helpful personality, as well as the personalities of her daughters. What I didn't know yet, but was thrilled to learn, was that Jona was also a talented seamstress—and she lived within a mile of me. It was friendship destiny.

Using a combination of my fabrics, Jona put together a darling skirt-and-shirt ensemble for my daughter, including a delicate spritz of embroidery at the hem of the skirt and a lavish amount of smocking. The detail and handwork were truly impressive. I was enchanted—as was little Charlotte as she spun in circles in her new outfit.

Many years have passed since that day, and I've spent much time with Jona and her excellent family. Jona has become one of my closest friends—and a delightful component of that friendship is our shared love of fabric and sewing. She has an eye for charming prints and playful details. From clothing and accessories to quilts and chair covers, Jona brings

flair to everything she makes. Her home brims with color and life. Her honesty and insight are an advantage to everyone who knows her. And her five children are enchantingly well behaved. We should all have such a talented, enthusiastic, and kindhearted friend to call on.

I am thrilled that Jona and her ideas are now available to you as well—in the form of this book. May you come to love her as I have and take delight in creativity as you explore the art of the A-line skirt.

XO, Heather Bailey

Contents

Introduction

Unlike many sewists, I did not learn to sew at my mother's knee. In junior high school I took a discouraging home economics course from an unenthused teacher, and although I learned a few basics, I certainly did not catch the "sewing bug." Nor did I finish sewing the poncho pattern I had chosen as my project (yes, poncho ... it was the 70s, after all). Four years later, I decided to brave another sewing attempt, and my mother indulged me by buying a few of yards of hot pink taffeta and a way-above-my-skill-set dress pattern. I didn't finish that project either, but this time my eyes were opening to the idea of all the amazing things that could come from a piece of fabric and a spool of thread.

Over time I developed a real knack for recognizing "good bones" in a seemingly plain commercial sewing pattern and turning it into something out of the ordinary and eye-catching. I had a great home-sewn work wardrobe. And then when I became a mother, I transferred those skills to my daughters' wardrobes and into my small children's clothing company, called Wiggle Wear, in my hometown of Portland, Oregon.

Many years (and a move to Arizona) later, I began writing my blog Stop Staring and Start Sewing! in the hopes that other sewists (or want-to-be sewists) would be inspired to get up from their computers and try to sew a few simple things. The response was beyond encouraging. Readers were actually following my advice to stop staring and start sewing.

A few years ago I began posting tutorials on my blog showing readers how I had turned a plain straight skirt pattern into an A-line skirt pattern and then added ruffles and other embellishments. I received so many enthusiastic comments from people re-creating those designs that I soon realized it wasn't just me—the A-line seemed to be everyone's favorite skirt style. I also received two critical comments (yes, they stung a little) and used those critiques as motivation to really research and understand what made a great skirt come together in a smart way with a flattering fit.

This book isn't my attempt to reinvent the wheel (or skirt), but an attempt to open sewists' eyes to all the great possibilities that can be found in one simple pattern. An A-line skirt can be professional or casual, classic or whimsical, simple or elaborate, colorful or muted—and that's with one pattern! All you need are a great-fitting pattern and a few simple skills, which are all covered in this book.

If you simply re-created the patterns featured in this book, you would have a large and varied wardrobe of skirts for every occasion. But don't feel bound by my examples; when you've got the hang of things, go ahead and mix and match layers, fabrics, hem variations, and trims and embellishments, and create your own original pieces. The possibilities are nearly endless, and new fabrics are always being released so you may never run out of ideas.

The A-line skirt is truly a classic skirt. It has been in style for more than 50 years, and I'm convinced it will still be a favorite 50 years from now. With this book and some great fabrics, you can create a beautiful and flattering wardrobe that will stand the test of time.

Jona Giammalva

Tools and Notions

A WELL-STOCKED SEWING KIT

A smart sewing kit is easy to put together and very reasonably priced. You'll need this basic supply list to get started, and then you can continue to add to the kit as you develop more sewing skills. I keep a wish list in my head and take advantage of sales to buy the more expensive items like good scissors or rotary cutter blades.

Tools for Measuring

1. FLEXIBLE MEASURING TAPE This is an absolute must-have for your sewing kit. I keep a long flexible measuring tape draped over a peg on the wall and a retractable measuring tape in my purse.

2. HEM GAUGE This inexpensive little gadget makes it so easy to get a perfectly even hem— plus you can use the edge to get nice, straight lines for darts and other small things that need tracing. Simply slide the plastic part to the ½″ (or whichever number you need) mark and use to mark hems an even ½″ all the way around your garment.

3. CLEAR PLASTIC QUILTING RULER I keep my 2″ × 18″ transparent ruler within arm's reach at all times. I use it with my rotary cutter to cut all the fabric strips for ruffles, bias tape, and anything else that is a long, straight line. I hang mine by the hole at one end on a bulletin board next to my cutting area.

Tools for Cutting

1. SCISSORS If you're just getting started sewing, then the cheap plastic-handled scissors are fine, but eventually you'll want to invest in a good pair of metal scissors. I use my 6″ Ginghers most often, and with regular sharpening, they stay in good-as-new condition. If you use your scissors for cutting anything other than fabric (e.g., paper), they will lose their sharp edge quickly, so be sure to have a special "fabric only" pair of scissors.

2. SNIPS Snips are tiny, pointy scissors that are great for small, detailed cutting. I use mine to snip the threads as I'm sewing through a project. They're also perfect for marking notches in the fabric as you're cutting a pattern out. A lot of smart folks keep them hanging from a retractable lanyard around their neck so they are always handy.

3. ROTARY CUTTER/MAT When it comes to cutting out patterns, a 45mm rotary cutter and self-healing mat are my tools of choice. You can find self-healing mats, with 1″ grids, in a variety of sizes, and they will last for years. The rotary blade, however, needs to be changed more often and should always be handled with caution. Even the simple act of brushing your hand up against it can draw blood, so always retract the blade when you're finished cutting and keep it out of the reach of children. When cutting, be sure to clear everything off the mat except the fabric because one run-in with an object, like a pin, will permanently damage the blade.

4. SEAM RIPPER I have at least three seam rippers on my sewing table at all times and get lots of use out of them. They're such nifty little gadgets, with the pointed end for picking threads and wayward stitches and the sharp blade tucked safely in the curved area. Seam rippers are so inexpensive that you can treat yourself to a nice, beefy, ergonomic one, such as Alex Anderson's 4-in-1 Essential Sewing Tool, and still not spend a lot of money.

Tools for Marking

1. WATER-SOLUBLE MARKER Water-soluble markers are great for marking on fabrics. They come in blue, for lighter fabrics, and white, for dark fabrics. The marks can be easily removed using a quick wipe with a damp cloth (or a simple squirt of water on fabrics that don't need special care). The marks from some ink become permanent from the heat of an iron, so read the package carefully. The markers can dry out quickly, so always remember to put the cap back on when you're done.

2. TRACING PAPER AND TRACING WHEEL Tracing paper comes in a pack with a variety of colors and is a wonderful tool for tracing lines and markings onto fabric with the tracing wheel. One package of tracing paper will last for years. I have a folder just for my tracing paper. I keep the tracing wheel in the folder pocket so that it's always with the paper when I need it.

3. PENCIL Although it's nice to have professional marking tools, a pencil is great in a pinch as long as you use it to mark in a place that won't be seen, like the seam allowance area.

Tools for Pressing

1. IRON If you do a lot of sewing (or laundry, for that matter) it's imperative that you have a decent iron. When shopping for a new iron, I start by looking for anything with steam and 1,600 watts or more (the wattage information is usually in small print on the back of the box). Anything less than 1,600 watts just doesn't have the heat to really work out the wrinkles and creases in most fabrics.

2. IRONING BOARD You probably already own an ironing board, but if you're in the market for a new one I recommend an ironing board with a metal iron holster attached to the end for holding the iron (even when it's hot).

Tools for Sewing

1. SEWING MACHINE WITH MANUAL I know this one seems obvious but I can't overemphasize the importance of having the manual for your sewing machine. I keep mine in a pocket on the wall right next to my sewing table, and I refer to it at least once a day. If you aren't the original owner of the machine, or have lost the manual, it's easy to find one online.

2. SEWING MACHINE NEEDLES Most needles are sized 8/60 (the 8 is the American size and the 60 is the European size) through 19/120. A size 8/60 needle is good for very lightweight and sheer fabrics; a size 19/120 needle is appropriate for a heavy fabric such as outdoor canvas material. I recommend a size 11/75 needle for most sewing projects using light- or medium-weight fabrics. For denim use a size 12/80 or 14/90.

3. HAND-SEWING NEEDLES It's good to have a nice assortment of hand-sewing needles for sewing on buttons and other embellishments.

4. THREAD I've used Coats & Clark Dual Duty thread for years. It's available in every shade of every color and has always performed great in all my garment sewing. For topstitching, you can use the same thread as you're using in your skirt, but you may want to try topstitching thread. It's a heavier thread, so a topstitching needle (which has a larger eye for the thread) is recommended as well.

5. INVISIBLE ZIPPER FOOT An invisible zipper foot is different from a regular zipper foot because it has grooves in the bottom for the zipper teeth to slide through and it allows the needle to get much closer to the teeth than a regular zipper foot does. If your machine didn't come with an invisible zipper foot, you can find one at a store that specializes in your brand of sewing machine (or online). If you're not ready to invest in a new foot, the people at Coats & Clark make an inexpensive plastic invisible zipper foot that can be adapted to any type of machine.

6. EDGE-STITCH FOOT / BLIND-HEM FOOT When you're topstitching or edgestitching, you want the stitch to be perfectly parallel to the seam for a clean, professional finish. Both the edge-stitch foot and the blind-hem foot (used with a straight stitch, not the blind-hem stitch) will allow you to do this with ease.

7. STRAIGHT PINS I use lots and lots of straight pins when sewing. They keep my seams lined up and stop the fabric from shifting while I'm sewing. I like to use the 1½"-long pins because they are easy to work with (and the ones with the pearlized heads are pretty). The long pins are great with cotton fabric, but if you are using a fine fabric such as silk or organza, you'll want to have smaller or extra-fine pins, which are less likely to leave holes.

8. PINCUSHION I love my magnetic pin holders. They're great for a quick pickup if your pins are on the floor. But it's also nice to have a cute little pincushion around just to keep your pins looking pretty.

SKIRT
FRONT

SIZE
SMALL

SKIRT
BACK

SIZE
SMALL

Place on fold.

THE *Pattern*

Tracing Your Pattern

Note: The master pattern is on pattern pullout pages P1–P4. Match the top and bottom halves of both the Skirt Front (labeled 1) and the Skirt Back (labeled 2) pattern pieces along the join lines before tracing and altering the pattern. Refer to the measurement chart (page 22) to find your pattern size.

Trace the assembled Skirt Front and Skirt Back pattern pieces onto your preferred pattern paper (page 23). After you've chosen a skirt style and fabric (or muslin if you are making a test skirt), you're ready to trace the pattern onto fabric.

Fold the fabric lengthwise, wrong sides together, and place the pattern piece along the folded edge, following the cutting layouts on this page or in the project instructions. You may need to place one pattern piece printed-side-down on the fabric to align both pieces on the fold, to orient the print correctly, or for a fabric with nap such as velvet or corduroy. Use pins or pattern weights to hold the paper pattern in place on the fabric.

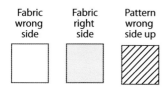

| Fabric wrong side | Fabric right side | Pattern wrong side up |

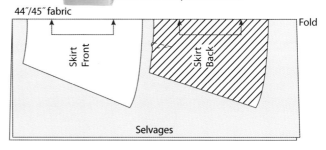

Basic Skirt (with no tucks/pleats in front)
44″/45″ fabric

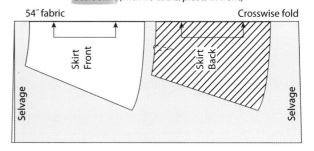

Basic Skirt (with no tucks/pleats in front)
54″ fabric

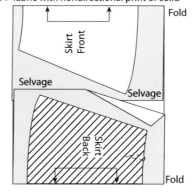

54″ fabric with nondirectional print or solid

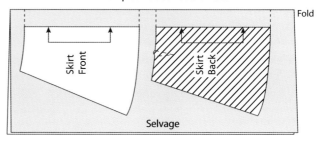

Skirt with pleats added to the front

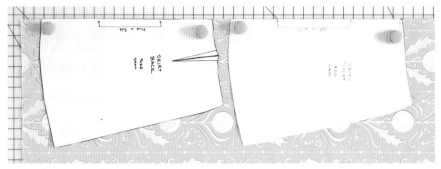

Pattern layout on 45″ fabric width

Slide a piece of tracing paper between the pattern and the fabric with the colored side against the fabric. (Unfold the tracing paper so you can use the whole length of it if necessary.)

If you're cutting out the whole skirt from the same fabric and not adding any other pieces to it, just trace along the pattern lines. Use the cutting line stated in the project instructions or choose your ideal length. The ½″ seam allowance is included.

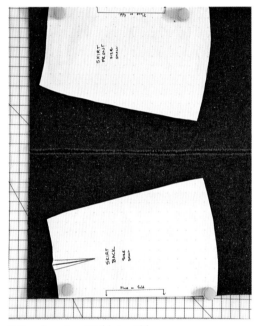

Pattern layout on 54″ fabric width

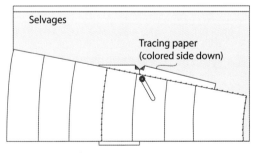

Trace on cutting lines.

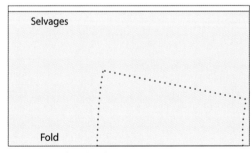

Pattern transferred to fabric

If you are making a skirt that uses one of the cutting lines marked on the interior of the pattern (for example, tier D on the Contrast Layer skirt, page 60), you will need to add a ½″ seam allowance to the upper and lower edges of the new section of the skirt.

Trace just the section you need onto the fabric.

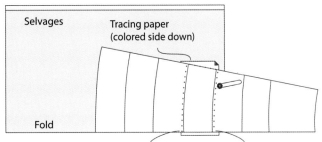

Trace a section of the pattern.

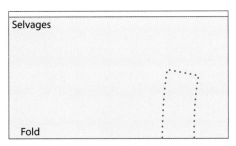

Partial pattern transferred to fabric

A second option is to make two master paper patterns and cut one of them into pieces along lines A–G. Be sure to mark each piece carefully (piece C, piece D, etc.). You'll still need to add a ½″ seam allowance when cutting, but you can bypass tracing onto the fabric this way.

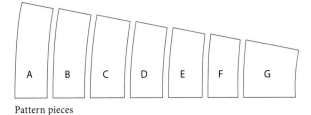

Pattern pieces

You'll still need to make a second copy or trace individual sections for the Contrast Pleat, Take 10, and Make It Maternity skirts, because these skirts are divided into even more sections.

GETTING THE *Right* FIT

Where to Measure

The nice thing about a book on skirts is that you really only need one measurement to find the right size for your body. Measure around your hips at the widest part (make sure your measuring tape is level and not riding up in the back), and use the chart to determine the right pattern size. If you are between sizes, pick the larger of the two because it's better to start with extra room than with too little.

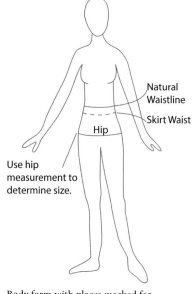

Natural Waistline

Skirt Waist

Hip

Use hip measurement to determine size.

Body form with places marked for measuring for size

U.S. Women's Sizes

Note: All measurements are inches.

	X-Small	Small	Medium	Large	X-Large
Sizes	2–4	6–8	10–12	14–16	18–20
Bust	32–34	34–35	36–37½	39–40½	42–44
Waist	22–25½	26½–27½	28½–30	31½–33	34½–36½
Hip	33–36½	37½–38½	39½–41	42½–44	45½–47½

Playing with Darts

Darts are a great way of making sure your skirt curves in along the places where your body curves in. The darts in the skirt pattern can be altered using a simple rule: The bigger the bump, the deeper the dart. If you have a round bottom you may need to make the darts higher and deeper than the darts on the pattern. If your bottom is on the flat side you will need the darts to be lower and shallower than the darts on the pattern. These are easy adjustments to make as you work on getting the perfect fit for your shape. Don't forget to write the changes on your pattern or make notes in this book as you're working the bugs out.

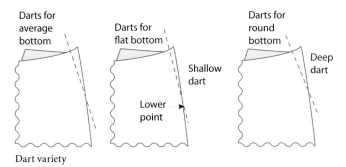

Dart variety

Adjusting the Waist

Since this skirt pattern is designed to have the skirt sit about 1″ below the waist, making alterations is very simple.

If you have a curvy figure you may want to curve the top waist of the pattern in, as shown in the diagram, based on your measurement 1″ below your waist, on both skirt front and skirt back patterns. Likewise, if you have a straighter waist simply draw a line up from the side, removing the curve from the pattern.

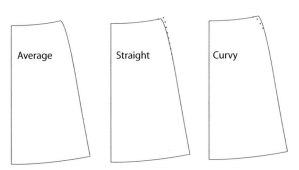

Making the Master Pattern

When you've made adjustments to the pattern so that it fits your shape comfortably (and you've tested it by sewing with muslin or practice fabric), you'll want to transfer the changes and additional markings onto a "master pattern." This is the pattern you will use for all your skirts. I have mine on a big piece of vellum from the craft store, but you can use Pellon's pattern paper (with or without grids) or even tissue wrap if you're in a pinch or want to get started.

Skirt BASICS

All the skirts in this book use the basic skirt construction techniques covered in this chapter.

The projects contain many design variations but will all be assembled in this fashion after you've made any embellishments such as pleats, tucks, and so on.

Please very carefully read the instructions for the style of skirt you've chosen before assembling it. Following the instructions for pattern placement (page 18), cut the pattern out and transfer any markings necessary for the skirt design you picked. Sew the front of the skirt completely (adding any pleats, etc.) and set it aside.

All seam allowances are ½″ unless otherwise noted.

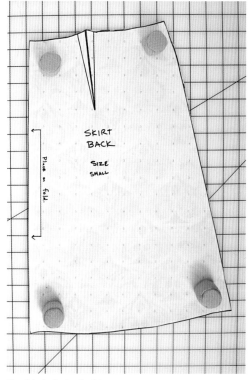

Cut fabric for basic skirt.

Yardage Requirements

After you've determined which length and style of skirt you will be sewing, the yardage requirements are easy to figure out. You'll find these lines on the pattern pullout.

Some skirts use the cutting lines to create tiers that are cut and sewn out of different fabrics than the main body of the skirt.

For each tier added to any skirt style: ⅜ yard

* Additional yardage may be required to match stripes, plaids, or one-way designs.

For 44″/45″ WOF, including a bit extra, you will need the following amounts:*

For the longest skirt
(cutting line A): 1⅞ yards

For cutting line B: 1⅝ yards

For cutting line C: 1⅓ yards

For cutting line D: 1¼ yards

For cutting line E: ⅞ yard

For cutting line F: ⅔ yard

Darts

If you're making a skirt with pleats in the back, please refer to those instructions and bypass these dart instructions.

MARKING DARTS

1. With the paper pattern piece still in place on the cut fabric, mark the darts on the Skirt Back piece by sliding a piece of tracing paper (folded so the colored side faces out on both sides) between the layers of the folded Skirt Back. Use a tracing wheel and straightedge ruler to trace the lines onto the wrong side of the fabric.

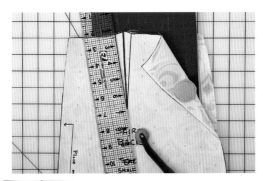
Trace darts.

2. Unfold the Skirt Back piece and check to make sure all the marks are easily visible.

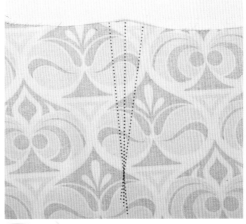
Visible darts

SEWING DARTS

1. Fold along the center dart line, right sides together, and press. The 2 outer lines should match up. Pin along the lines and check both sides to make sure the pins are going through the lines on both sides. Press.

Press darts.

2. Sew the darts along the outer line, starting at the upper edge of the skirt back.

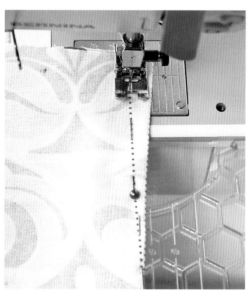

Sew darts.

3. When you've reached the point of the dart, do *not* backstitch (this could leave an unsightly pucker on the other side of the skirt). Sew off the edge of the fold and either cut the thread with a 5″ tail and tie a knot by hand or, even quicker, run a few stitches back and forth just above the point in the folded area of the pleat (where it won't show on the outside).

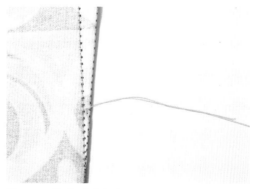

Sew lock stitch inside dart.

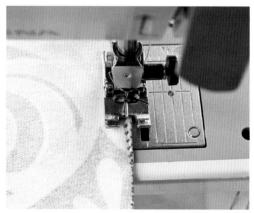

Close-up of lock stitch in dart

4. Press the darts first as you sewed them and then toward the center of the skirt back.

Skirt Assembly

1. Pin the skirt front and back pieces together at the sides along the ½″ seamline and try on to check the fit.

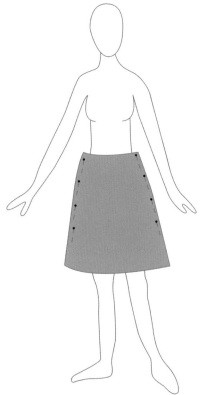

Pin skirt on for size.

2. Make any necessary adjustments at the darts or sides. (Don't forget to make a note of these changes on the pattern and in the note section for each skirt.) Now install the invisible zipper (page 33) and sew the side seam of the skirt on that side, using a ½″ seam allowance. Finish the seam allowances by serging or zigzag stitching along the raw edges. Press the seam open from the inside and press again from the outside.

3. After the zipper is installed, sew the other side of the skirt together using a ½″ seam allowance. Finish the seam allowances and press as in Step 2.

Sew other side of skirt.

4. Hem the skirt using the method of your choice detailed in the hem section (page 40).

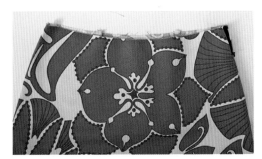

Finished basic skirt before lining

5. Now install the lining, following the lining instructions (page 28).

6. Press your skirt one last time, and you're finished!

Adding the Lining

Most skirt patterns include a facing to finish the waist, but I love to take it a simple step further and include a lining in my skirts. Lining a skirt is practical for so many reasons. First, it adds a nice, solid backing, especially when the skirt is made from lightweight fabric (no peekaboos). Second, it saves you the trouble of having to look for a slip or hearing those dreaded words, "It's snowing down south." And third, as you'll learn in this book, a lining can be a very versatile design element, which gives each new skirt a completely different look than the last.

MAKING THE LINING

1. To make a basic lining for your skirt, simply use the skirt pattern pieces just as you did when sewing the skirt. Cut the lining shorter than the skirt by using the next cutting line up from the cutting line you used at the bottom of the skirt (example: if the skirt stops at cutting line C, cut the lining at cutting line D).

2. Stitch the darts in the back of the lining the same way you did in the skirt back and press the darts first as you sewed them and then toward the center.

3. Pin both lining pieces together with the right sides facing each other. With the skirt back piece facing you, stitch the right side together using a ½″ seam allowance. Now stitch up the left side, stopping 9″ from the top and back-stitching (this leaves an opening for the zipper).

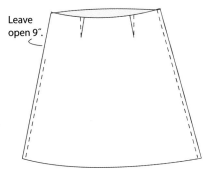

Pin and stitch lining side seams.

4. Use scissors to snip the seam allowances in toward the point where you backstitched, but be sure you don't snip through the seam.

5. Fold the raw edges over ½″ at the zipper opening and press. Finish the raw seam allowances on both sides (except for the folded part) using a serger or zigzag stitch.

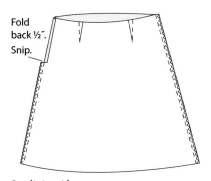

Sew lining sides.

6. Hem the lower edge of the lining using a rolled hem stitch on your serger, or following the Basic ½″ Hem instructions, using a ¼″ fold (page 40). Press all the seams on the lining well before attaching it in the next step.

Alternate Lining Method

Here is an alternate method to assemble the skirt lining, with a few extra steps that ensure a perfect finish. By sewing the lining this way, you still get the soft, finished part of the lining against your hips without the seam facing outward at the bottom of the lining, where it might be seen.

1. Follow Making the Lining, Steps 1 and 2 (page 28).

2. Pin and sew the lining front and back pieces together at the sides, stopping 9″ short of the bottom and remembering to leave the zipper opening.

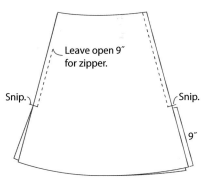

Sew lining sides partially.

3. Snip the seam allowances, being careful not to cut into the stitches, at the stopping point. Turn the lining right side out. Flip the remaining seam so it is now facing outward and, starting at the point where you stopped previously, continue sewing the seam all the way to the bottom.

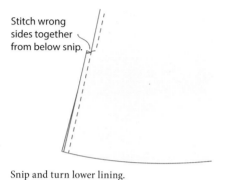

Stitch wrong sides together from below snip.

Snip and turn lower lining.

4. Finish the seams on both sides with your serger or a zigzag stitch and refer to Making the Lining, Steps 4–6 (page 29), to complete the lining.

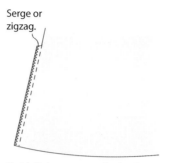

Serge or zigzag.

Finish lining seams on both sides.

ATTACHING THE LINING TO THE SKIRT

1. Slip the skirt lining, wrong side out, over the skirt, right side out, until the top edges and side seams are aligned with each other. Pin the lining to the skirt, starting at the right side (where the skirt and lining side seams are facing each other) and ending at the zipper. Make any adjustments to the lining's zipper opening so the folded edge is right next to the zipper (about ¼″ from the teeth). You may need to adjust the folded lining edge and press it again.

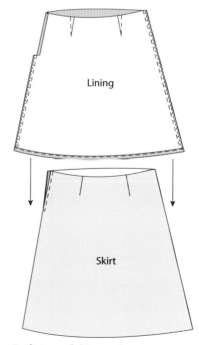

Lining

Skirt

Put lining and skirt together.

2. Sew the skirt and lining together all the way around the top using a ½″ seam allowance.

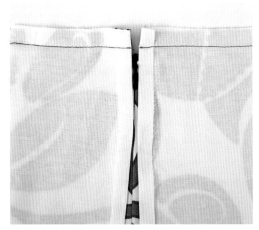

Sew lining and skirt together.

Open the seam up and inspect the zipper area to make sure both sides are even at the top where they end.

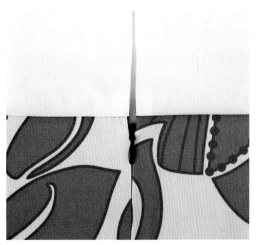

Check to make sure sides match.

3. Press the seam allowance toward the lining and, from the right side of the lining, topstitch ⅛″ from the seam through the lining and the seam allowance. This is called understitching, and it helps the lining stay in place.

Understitch lining.

4. Now tack the lining's zipper opening to the zipper tape using a simple slip stitch.

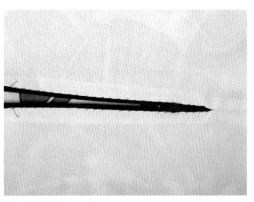

Slipstitch lining to zipper.

You now have a lined skirt! Use this method to attach the linings on all the skirts in this book. In the skirt projects to come, I will show you all the fun things you can do with the lower lining.

TECHNIQUES FOR A *Beautiful* FINISH

Add Appliqué

SUPPLIES

- Fusible web such as HeatnBond (specifically for fabric—follow the manufacturer's instructions)
- Contrasting fabric
- Contrasting thread

Making an appliqué is fun and very easy. Choose a solid fabric and draw any shape you like on it, or use printed fabric and choose one of the designs on that print. Iron a big enough piece of fusible web to the wrong side of the appliqué fabric. When it has cooled, cut out your desired shape. Iron the appliqué where you want it on the skirt. Using a small zigzag stitch, sew all the way around the outer edge of the appliqué, securing it to the fabric. It is easiest to do this just after you've sewn the skirt front and back together.

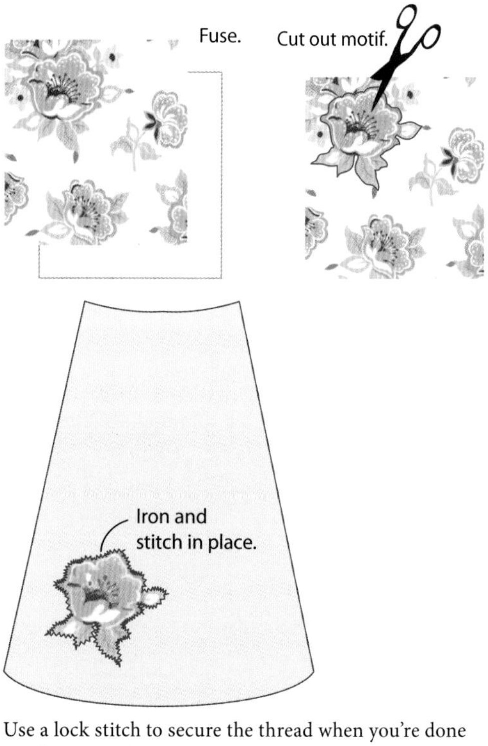

Fuse.
Cut out motif.
Iron and stitch in place.

Use a lock stitch to secure the thread when you're done or, if your machine doesn't do a lock stitch, pull all the threads through to the back of the fabric and tie them together in a tight little knot.

Install an Invisible Zipper

I love invisible zippers! They add such a clean, professional look to clothes and are deceptively simple to install. On some machines a regular zipper foot will work if you can move the needle right next to the zipper teeth. Some regular zipper feet also have a groove in the bottom to get the zipper closer to the needle.

If you want an invisible zipper foot but you're not sure about investing in one, Coats & Clark makes an inexpensive, adaptable, invisible zipper foot.

These instructions are for installing a 7″–9″ zipper on the left side of the skirt.

1. After you've sewn the darts in the skirt back, finish the edges of the skirt pieces by serging or zigzagging along the length of the skirt pieces on the side where the zipper will be (with the right side of the fabric facing you, finish the left side of the skirt back and the right side of the skirt front). Figure A

A. Finish edges to prep for zipper.

2. Prepare the zipper by opening it up all the way and pressing the edges with your iron (push the iron into the zipper teeth to "unfold" the crease). Figure B

3. On the skirt back, place the zipper face-down with the left side of the zipper against the edge of the skirt piece. Pin it so the upper zipper stop is ¾″ from the top edge of the skirt and the zipper teeth are ½″ from the side. Figure C

B. Press zipper.

C. Pin zipper on side of skirt back.

4. Baste the zipper in place by machine or by hand. This step keeps the zipper from shifting while you sew it in place. When you're done you can remove the basting threads if you want, but nobody will see them so it's okay if you want to leave them there. Figure D

D. Baste zipper on side of skirt back.

5. Lower the invisible zipper foot so the right groove is over the zipper teeth and the needle is just to the side on the left. Sew the zipper in place along the side of the zipper teeth. Be sure not to sew into the teeth (the zipper won't slide completely if there is a stitch in the way). Figure E

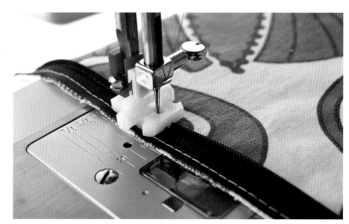

E. Sew zipper in place on skirt back piece.

6. Stitch as far down as you can go before the foot bumps against the back of the zipper pull at the bottom. You'll probably stop about 1″–2″ short of the bottom of the zipper, and that's fine. Figure F

7. Close and open the zipper just to make sure it's working smoothly.

F. Stop stitching near bottom of zipper.

G. Pin zipper to skirt front piece.

H. Baste zipper on skirt front piece.

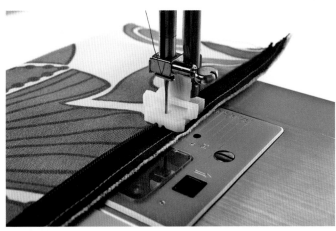

I. Sew zipper in place on skirt front piece.

8. Pin the other side of the zipper to the right side of the skirt front. Figure G

9. Baste the zipper to the right side of the skirt front just as you did on the first side. Figure H

10. Lower the invisible zipper foot so the left groove is over the zipper teeth and the needle is on the right side of the teeth. Sew the zipper in place along the side of the zipper teeth, stopping at the same level as on the first side. Figure I

11. Close the zipper and give it a good inspection before moving on to the next step.

When you're done you can remove the basting threads if you want, but nobody will see them so it's okay if you want to leave them there.

Close zipper and check your work.

12. To close the remaining side seam, pinch the area to be sewn together with the bottom tails of the zipper poking out between the seam allowances. Pin through all 4 layers (this keeps the seam allowance out of the way while you sew along the zipper). Pin the rest of the skirt sides together normally all the way to the bottom.

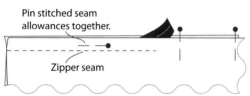

Pinch zipper between seam allowance and pin through layers.

13. Start stitching about ½″ above the spot where the zipper stitching ends. Sew as close to the zipper as possible (right next to the zipper's stitch line), and keep sewing all the way to the bottom of the skirt, using a ½″ seam allowance.

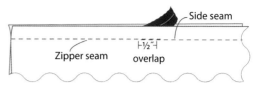

Stitch next to lower part of zipper all the way down seam.

14. Press the seam open from inside the skirt, being careful not to iron over the zipper teeth.

15. Press the seam on the outside of the skirt. In fact, you'll want to be sure to press each seam open (or to the side if your seam allowances are serged together) after it is sewn.

Your zipper is in and you're ready for the next step!

Topstitching and Edgestitching

TOPSTITCHING

Topstitching is a nice way to give your seams a professional, finished look. It also helps maintain the integrity of the seam by holding the seam allowance down. (And as an extra bonus, it helps make ironing so much simpler.) You may want to try thread made especially for topstitching with a top-stitching needle for a really nice top stitch. If you have an edge-stitch foot or a blind-hem foot (used with a straight stitch setting), this will help guide the fabric to keep your stitching line straight. I like to use a stitch length of 2.5–3 for topstitching.

Before you topstitch, press the seam allowance to the side on the wrong side of the fabric. Turn the fabric over and topstitch directly above the seam allowance just to the side of the seam. The stitch should be close enough to the seam (less than ¼″) to sew through the seam allowance.

How to topstitch (close up)

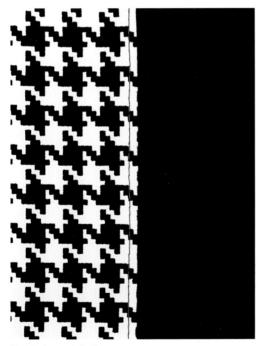

Finished topstitched seam

EDGESTITCHING

Edgestitching is a great way to stitch a fold so it becomes crisp and permanent. Like the top stitch, it also looks professional and makes ironing much easier. If you have an edge-stitch foot or a blind-hem foot, this will help guide the stitch to keep it straight. I like to use a stitch length of 2.5–3 for edgestitching.

To edgestitch, simply sew a line as close to the fold as possible (about ⅛″ away).

Edgestitching on fold

Belt Loops

Belt loops are a nice feature if you want to add a sash or ribbon to your skirt. With belt loops, you can change the look of the skirt simply by switching the color of the sash.

1. Cut a rectangle of fabric 1″ × 12″.

2. Fold the fabric in half lengthwise and press. Open it back up, fold the edges to the middle crease, and press again. Now fold it again so the folded strip of fabric is ¼″ wide. Figure A

3. Edgestitch along both edges of the folded fabric. Figure B

A. Belt loop fabric folded twice

B. Edgestitch both sides.

4. Cut the sewn strip into 3 equal pieces, each ¼″ × 4″.

5. Place the loop ½″ away from the zipper on the back piece of the skirt. Slide the top of the loop so that it's 2¾″ from the top of the skirt. Mark the loop 3″ down from the top of the skirt and pin in place.

6. Now stitch across the loop fabric at the 3″ point. Figure C

7. Flip the loop up toward the top of the skirt and stitch across the bottom of it (make sure the stitch is close enough to the bottom to stitch down the loose piece of loop fabric underneath). Stitch across the top ⅜″ from the edge. Figure D

8. Repeat Steps 5–7 to sew belt loops in the center back and on the other side of the skirt ½″ back from the seam. The top, raw edge of the belt loop will be hidden insdie the skirt when you attach the lining. Figure E

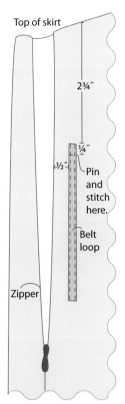

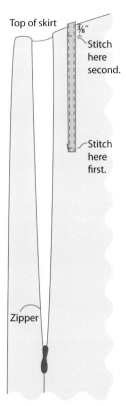

C. Pin and stitch loop in place at bottom.

D. Flip loop up and stitch across top.

E. Back belt loop centered and side loops

Choose Your Hem

BASIC ½″ HEM

Most of the skirts in this book have a basic ½″ hem. Simply fold the edge over ½″ using your hem gauge, press, fold another ½″, press, and then stitch.

Folding and pressing ½″ hem

Sewing ½″ hem

ROLLED HEM

A rolled hem is a nice, flowy way to finish a skirt edge. It looks best with natural fabrics such as linens and silks. Keep in mind that the skirt will be nearly 1″ longer with a rolled hem than with a ½″ hem, so you may want to cut 1″ off the bottom of the skirt before sewing the rolled hem.

Refer to your sewing machine manual to use the rolled-hem foot on your sewing machine or serger to get a good, clean rolled hem.

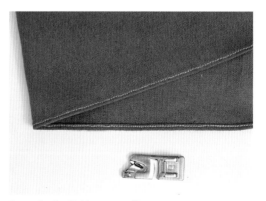
Example of rolled hem on ruffle

BIAS TAPE HEM

Another method used in this book is the bias tape hem. This is a fun way to make the hem stand out and/or coordinate with another element of the skirt. Feel free to use this on any of the skirts you're making, but keep in mind that the skirt will be ¾″ longer than the same skirt with the basic ½″ hem.

1. Measure around the skirt hem to determine the circumference of the skirt. This is the length of bias tape needed. Add at least 8″ to that number to give you some extra to work with. Cut the fabric for the bias tape on a 45° angle to the grain (on the bias). Cut each strip 2″ wide (the clear 2″ ruler comes in handy for this process). Figure A

2. Overlap the ends of the strips, leaving a ¼″ seam allowance. Sew across the strips where they intersect forming a V. Figure B

3. Press the seams open and snip off the little corners (called dog ears) that are sticking out from the sides. Figure C

4. Fold the bias tape in half lengthwise, wrong sides together, and press. Figure D

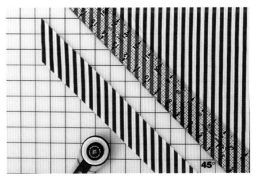

A. Cut bias fabric for bias hem.

B. Sew ends of bias strips together.

C. Press seams open and snip corners.

D. Fold and press in half.

5. Aligning the raw edges, pin the bias tape to the edge of your skirt hem on the wrong side (yes!). Figure E

6. Sew around using a ⅜″ seam allowance, but leave a gap of about 3″ at the beginning and end to join the bias tape together.

7. Open the bias tape at the unstitched ends and fold the ends back where they meet. Press well. Figure F

8. Using the fold as your stitching line, sew the ends of the bias tape together. Trim the seam allowance to ¼″ and press it open. Figure G

9. Fold the bias tape in half and finish stitching it to the skirt so the gap is now closed. Figure H

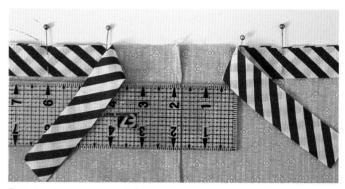

E. Pin in place on wrong side, leaving opening.

F. Sew bias on, and fold back open ends.

G. Sew ends together using fold as guide.

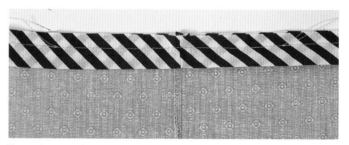

H. Finish sewing bias on wrong side.

I. Press bias away from wrong side.

J. Fold bias over to right side, press, and pin.

10. Fold the bias tape over the stitching line toward the raw edge of the skirt hem and press. Figure I

11. Fold the bias tape over to the right side of the skirt. Press well and pin in place. Figure J

12. Sew in place close to the edge. Figure K

K. Sew bias in place.

RUFFLE HEM

Ruffles are such a cute, whimsical way to finish a hem and are so simple to make.

Determining Fabric Length for Ruffles

For a ruffled hem I like to use a 1:1.75 ruffle ratio. For example, if I'm adding a ruffle to a 100″ length of fabric (determined by measuring the circumference of the skirt's hem), I'll need a length of 175″ for the ruffle strip.

1. Cut enough WOF (width of fabric) strips to equal the length of ruffle strip you need, plus a little extra for seam allowances.

2. Sew the short ends of the strips together, pressing the seam allowances open, to make a big circle.

Ruffle Edge Finishes

The edges of the ruffles in this book can be finished three different ways, each of which changes the width you cut the unfinished ruffle strips.

1. For a rolled hem ruffle, just add the finished width to the seam allowance (so you'll need a 1¼″-wide cut strip for a 1″ wide finished ruffle) and roll the hem on one long edge, following the manufacturer's instructions for your sewing machine's rolled-hem foot.

2. For a ¼″ hemmed ruffle, add the seam allowance to the desired finished width plus ½″ for hemming. Fold one long edge under ¼″ twice before topstitching along the fold.

3. For a folded ruffle, simply add the desired finished width of the ruffle to the amount of the seam allowance and then double this number to get the width needed for the fabric strips. (Example: For a 1″ finished ruffle with a ¼″ seam allowance, add 1″ + ¼″ and then double to 2½″.) When the strips are sewn together into a loop, fold in half and press.

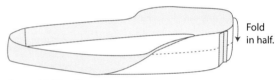

Fold in half.

Sew and fold ruffle strips.

Gathering Ruffles

1. After you've finished the ruffle edge, it's time to gather the ruffle. Set your machine at the longest stitch length possible (I set mine at 5) and sew around the unfinished edge of the ruffle ¼″ from the edge. Do *not* backstitch at either the start or finish of the stitch. Repeat this process, but this time stitch between the previous stitch and the unfinished edge of the ruffle.

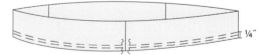

¼″

Folded ruffle with gathering stitches

2. Pull the gathering threads, adjusting the gathers evenly as you pull.

3. Pin the gathered ruffle to the bottom of the skirt, right sides and raw edges together. Pull the gathers and distribute them evenly as needed. This part is somewhat tedious, but if you take your time, you'll get a beautiful result. Wrap the loose thread end around a pin in a figure-8 motion to secure the gathers while you sew. Sew in place using a ¼″ seam.

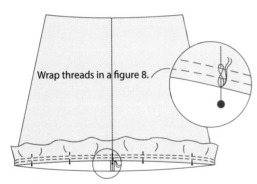

Attach ruffle to lower skirt.

4. Press the seam allowance upward and topstitch above the ruffle on the outside of the skirt.

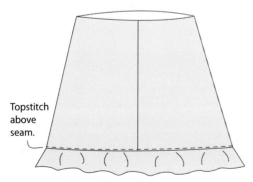

Finish topstitching ruffle on skirt.

Double-Edged Ruffles

Double-edged ruffles are not stitched as part of a seam but go on the outside of the skirt or lining. Add as many layers of these ruffles as you want.

Measure around the skirt where you want a ruffle. Multiply this number by 1.75 to determine the length of the ruffle. Cut enough strips 1″ wide × WOF out of the ruffle fabric to equal this length plus a little extra for seam allowances. Sew the short ends of the strips together to make a circle. Finish the edges by serging or using a small zigzag stitch. Sew a row of gathering stitches (I set my stitch length at 5) on each side of the center of the circle.

> If your machine has the option of moving the needle over, use that feature and simply set the needle to each side of the center as needed.

Pull the threads to gather the ruffles and pin them in place on your skirt. Stitch between the 2 gathering stitches. Pull out the gathering threads.

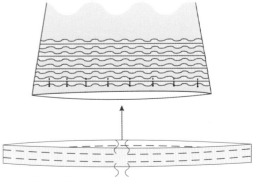

Pin double ruffles on skirt.

THE *Skirts*

This is the ultimate feminine skirt.

Feel free to use a funky fabric to give it sass because the sweet ruffle will give it enough daintiness to balance it out nicely. In this version I've used the same white fabric for the ruffle that I used for the lining, but you could use a fun print for the ruffle and get an entirely new look. You can choose to make it in a different length as well, but you may need to adjust the amount of bias trim and ruffle strips.

Cutting

Refer to Tracing Your Pattern (page 19) and Skirt Basics (page 24) to trace and cut the desired size and length of the Skirt Front and Skirt Back pattern pieces.

SKIRT FABRIC: Cut 1 Skirt Front on fold and 1 Skirt Back on fold.

LINING FABRIC: Cut 1 Skirt Front on fold and 1 Skirt Back on fold.

BIAS HEM FABRIC: Cut enough 2″-wide bias strips to make 75″ of continuous bias trim.

RUFFLE FABRIC: Cut the number of strips determined in Step 4 of Assembly 4½″ × WOF.

MASTER PATTERN MARKS

SKIRT LENGTH: Cutting line B

LINING LENGTH: Cutting line B

EXTRA SUPPLIES

FABRIC FOR BIAS HEM: ½ yard

FABRIC FOR LINING RUFFLE: ½ yard

Basic Skirt

WITH SWEET RUFFLE LINING

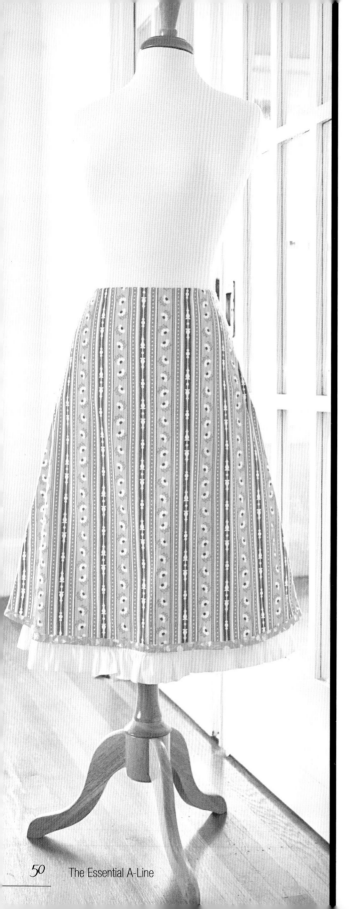

Assembly

Use a ½" seam allowance unless noted otherwise.

1. Assemble the skirt using the instructions in Skirt Basics (page 24).

2. Hem the skirt using the bias tape hem method (page 41).

3. When sewing the lining side seams, be sure to stop sewing about 9" from the bottom and flip the seam allowance the other direction as detailed in Alternate Lining Method (page 29). This way there's no chance that any seams will be seen as you're moving about in your skirt.

The lining will be the same length as the skirt, so just enough ruffle will peek out under the hem. I've used a 2" folded ruffle for this version, with a ¼" seam allowance, so my ruffle strips were cut 4½" wide and then folded and gathered.

4. Refer to Determining the Fabric Length for Ruffles (page 44) and Ruffle Edge Finishes (page 44) to measure the lining hem and make the appropriately sized ruffle loop.

5. Refer to Gathering Ruffles to gather and attach the ruffle hem to the lining, using a ¼" seam allowance.

6. Don't forget to press the ruffle seam allowance upward, and topstitch just above the seam on the right side of the fabric (page 36).

Notes

I call this *the Triple Ruffle skirt,* but *you can ruffle as many layers as you like* — make a Quadruple Ruffle skirt / or add even more ruffles! Mix and match the fabrics to make it extra fun, or use all the same fabrics for a more urbane look.

Cutting

Refer to Tracing Your Pattern (page 19) and the cutting layouts below and on page 54 to trace and cut the desired size of the Skirt Front and Skirt Back patterns onto your fabric. Be sure to add a ½" seam allowance on any edges that will be sewn to another skirt piece edge (except for the skirt sides).

RUFFLE FABRIC: Cut the number of strips determined in Step 3 of Assembly 3″ × WOF.

MAIN FABRIC:

45″ (115cm) fabric w/wo nap
XS–XL: 1¾ yards (1.6m)

54″ (135cm) fabric w/wo nap
L–XL: 1¾ yards (1.6m)

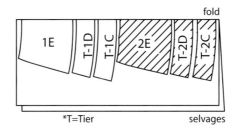

54″ (135cm) fabric w/wo nap
XS–M: 1⅜ yards (1.2m)

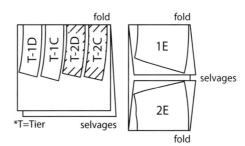

MASTER PATTERN MARKS

SKIRT LENGTH: Top to cutting line E, tier D, tier C (don't forget to add ½" seam allowances)

LINING LENGTH: Cutting line D

EXTRA SUPPLIES

FABRIC FOR RUFFLES: ⅝ yard for XS/S/M, ¾ yard for L/XL

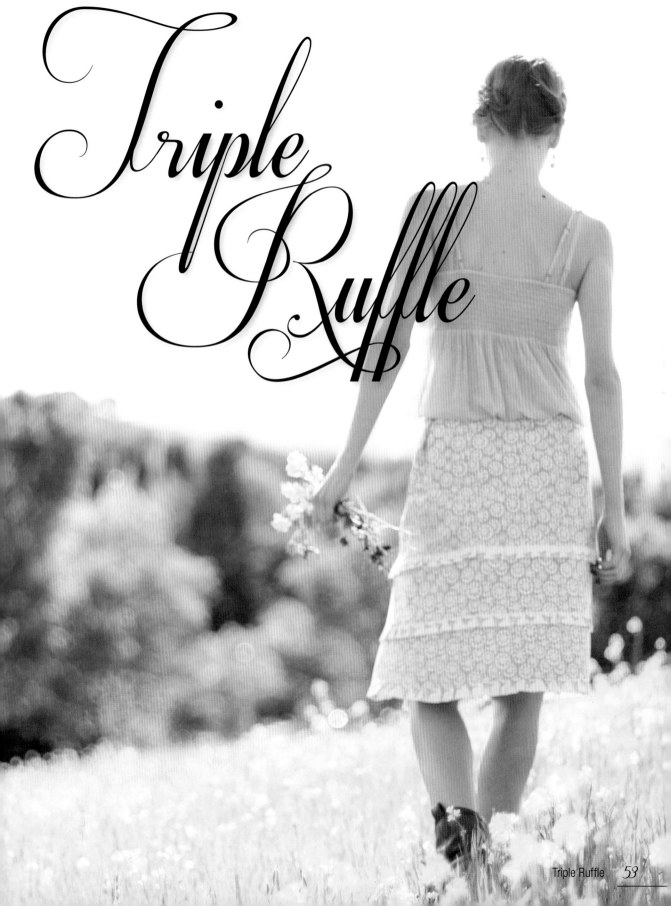

Triple Ruffle

45″ (115cm) lining
XS–XL: 1¼ yards (1.1m)

54″ (135cm) lining
M–XL: 1¼ yards (1.1m)

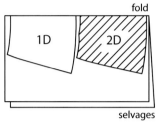

54″ (135cm) lining
XS–S: ¾ yards (0.7m)

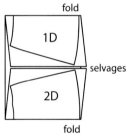

Assembly

Use a ½″ seam allowance unless noted otherwise.

1. Refer to Skirt Basics (page 24) to sew the top part of the skirt.

2. Sew the tier D front and back pieces, right sides together, at the sides. Press the seams open. Repeat with the tier C pieces. Repeat with any additional tiers.

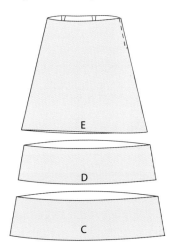

3. Refer to Determining the Fabric Length for Ruffles (page 44) and Ruffle Edge Finishes, Folded Ruffle (page 44), to measure the lower edge of the skirt top and each tier, cut ruffle strips, and make the appropriately sized ruffle loops.

4. Refer to Gathering Ruffles (page 44) to gather the ruffles for the upper skirt and pin in place at the lower edge. Sew using a ½″ seam allowance.

5. Sew tier D to the bottom of the upper skirt, right sides together.

6. Repeat Steps 4 and 5 to gather and attach the remaining ruffles and tiers.

7. Press all the seams upward and topstitch on the skirt fabric above each ruffle.

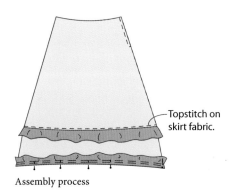

Topstitch on skirt fabric.

Assembly process

8. Finish your skirt by installing the lining (page 30).

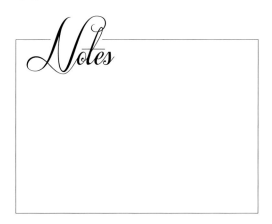

Notes

This skirt is so cute!

You can make it any length and add as many layers of ruffles as you like. You can make the ruffles out of a contrasting fabric or make each ruffle from a different fabric. Even a simple change, like using a bold thread on the ruffle edges, can add a fun twist to the skirt.

Cutting

Refer to Tracing Your Pattern (page 19) and Skirt Basics (page 24) to trace and cut out the desired size and length of the Skirt Front and Skirt Back patterns.

SKIRT FABRIC: Cut 1 Skirt Front on fold and 1 Skirt Back on fold.

LINING FABRIC: Cut 1 Skirt Front on fold and 1 Skirt Back on fold.

RUFFLE FABRIC: Cut the number of strips determined in Steps 2 and 3 of Assembly 1¼″ × WOF.

MASTER PATTERN MARKS

SKIRT LENGTH: Cutting line C

LINING LENGTH: Cutting line D

EXTRA SUPPLIES

FABRIC FOR RUFFLES: ⅜ yard

Applied Ruffle

Assembly

Use a ½″ seam allowance unless noted otherwise.

1. Refer to Skirt Basics (page 24) to sew the skirt.

2. Follow the diagram below to determine at what height to place the ruffles. Measure the circumference of the areas where you want to place the ruffles. Multiply that number by 1.5 to get the length needed for each ruffle loop.

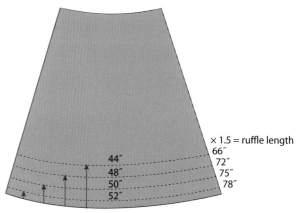

Mark levels and measure for applied ruffles.

3. Refer to Double-Edged Ruffles (page 45) to make 4 ruffle loops to the lengths you determined in Step 2.

Finish and gather applied ruffle.

4. Pull the gathering threads and adjust them while pinning the first ruffle around the skirt.

Pin ruffles.

5. Sew the first ruffle to the skirt by stitching between the gathering stitches. Remove the gathering threads.

Sew ruffles.

6. Repeat Steps 4 and 5 with all the remaining rows of ruffles.

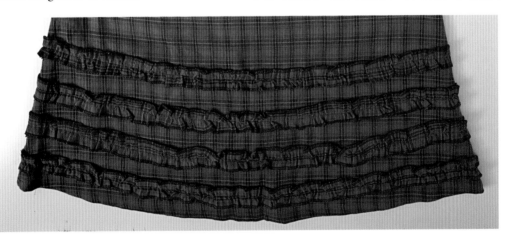

All ruffles sewn in place

7. Finish your skirt by installing the lining (page 30) and hemming with a basic ½″ hem (page 40).

This is one of my favorite skirts!

You can use large fabric scraps and mix it up like crazy. Each tier is a different fabric, and the thin bias strips between the layers add a dramatic punch. The ruffle at the bottom is small but significant. This version ends above the knee, but you can make as many layers as you like.

Cutting

Refer to Tracing Your Pattern (page 19) and the cutting layouts below to trace and cut the desired size and length of the Skirt Front and Skirt Back pattern pieces. Be sure to add a ½″ seam allowance on any edges that will be sewn to another skirt piece edge (except for the skirt sides).

BIAS TRIM AND RUFFLE FABRIC: Cut as many inches of 2″-wide strips on the bias as determined in Assembly, Step 3 (page 62), for bias trim. Cut as many strips 2″ × WOF as determined in Assembly, Step 3 (page 62), for ruffle.

FABRIC 1:

45″ (115cm) fabric w/wo nap
XS–XL: ¾ yard (0.7m)

54″ (135cm) fabric w/wo nap
XL: ¾ yard (0.7m)

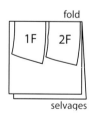

54″ (135cm) fabric w/wo nap
XS–L: ½ yard (0.4m)

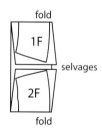

FABRIC 2, 3, AND 4 EACH:

45″ (115cm) fabric w/wo nap
XS–XL: ½ yard (0.4m)

54″ (135cm) fabric w/wo nap
XS–XL: ½ yard (0.4m)

*T=Tier

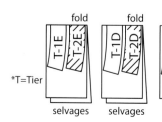

EXTRA SUPPLIES

Fabric for bias trim and ruffle hem: ¾ yard for XS/S, ⅞ yard for M/L/XL

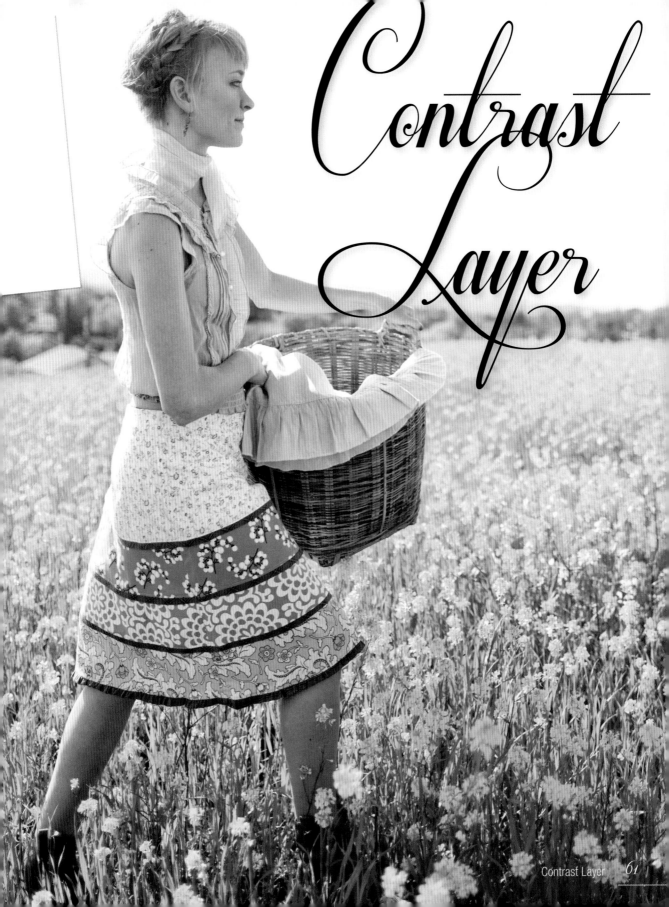

Contrast
Layer

LINING:

45″ (115cm) lining
XS–XL: 1¼ yards (1.1m)

54″ (135cm) lining
M–XL: 1¼ yards (1.1m)

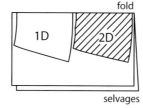

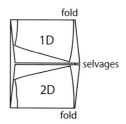

54″ (135cm) lining
XS–S: ¾ yard (0.7m)

Assembly

Use a ½″ seam allowance unless noted otherwise.

1. Refer to Skirt Basics (page 24) to sew the skirt top with the zipper.

2. Sew the front and back pieces of all the other tiers, right sides together, at the side seams.

3. Measure the circumference of the bottom edge of each tier to determine how much bias trim and ruffle fabric you will need. Refer to Bias Tape Hem, Steps 1–4 (page 41), to make enough bias strips to hem 3 tiers.

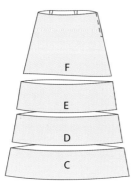

4. Pin the folded bias to the right side of the lower edge of the upper skirt, aligning the raw edges of both bias and skirt. Using a ⅜″ seam allowance, attach the bias tape to the bottom of the upper skirt, following Bias Tape Hem, Steps 5–9 (page 41) (just be sure you're sewing it to the right side of the skirt).

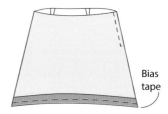

5. Pin Tier E to the bottom of the skirt. Sew in place with a ½″ seam allowance.

6. Repeat Steps 4 and 5 with all tiers.

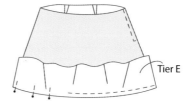

7. For the final tier, measure the circumference of the hem. Refer to Determining the Fabric Length for Ruffles (page 44) and Ruffle Edge Finishes, Folded Ruffle (page 44), to cut and assemble enough 2″ × WOF strips for the ruffle loop.

8. Refer to Gathering Ruffles (page 44) to gather the raw edge of the ruffle loop and sew the ruffle to the bottom of the skirt.

9. Press all the seam allowances upward and topstitch on the outside just above each tier.

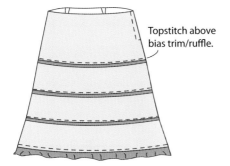

Topstitch above
bias trim/ruffle.

10. Refer to Skirt Basics (page 28) to make and install the lining in the usual fashion.

Notes

Try a variety of hems with a beautiful and versatile layered skirt. If you limit the contrast fabric to just the lower part of the lining, you might be able to use some smaller fabric pieces from your stash.

This layered skirt has a bias hem, but you can make it with a ruffled hem and even use different fabrics for each bias or ruffle layer. You also can choose any of the other lengths on the pattern—just make sure the lining is longer than the outer skirt.

Cutting

Refer to Tracing Your Pattern (page 19) and the cutting layouts (page 66) to trace and cut the desired size and length of the Skirt Front and Skirt Back patterns for the 2-part lining. Be sure to add a ½″ seam allowance at the top of the contrast lining fabric and the bottom of the upper lining fabric.

MASTER PATTERN MARKS

SKIRT LENGTH: Cutting line D

LINING LENGTH: Cutting line C (upper lining top to E, contrast lining tiers E to C)

Note: The lining is 1 tier longer than the outer skirt.

EXTRA SUPPLIES

FABRIC FOR BIAS HEM: ½ yard for XS, ⅝ yard for all other sizes

FABRIC FOR CONTRAST LINING: ¾ yard

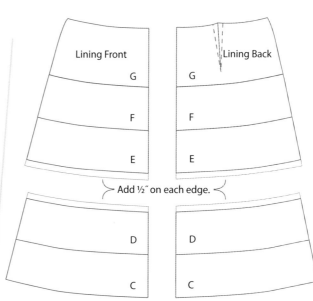

Alter paper pattern for lining only.

Layered
WITH Bias Hem

MAIN FABRIC:

45″ (115cm) fabric w/wo nap
XS–XL: 1¼ yards (1.1m)

54″ (135cm) fabric w/wo nap
M–XL: 1¼ yards (1.1m)

54″ (135cm) fabric w/wo nap
XS–S: ¾ yards (0.7m)

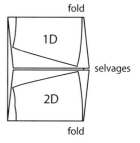

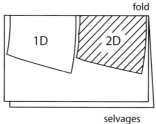

selvages

LOWER CONTRAST LINING:

45″–54″ (115–135cm) fabric
w/wo nap
XS–XL: ¾ yard (0.7m)

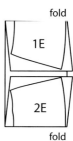

fold

*T=Tier

selvages

UPPER LINING:

45″ (115cm) lining
XS–XL: 1 yard (0.9m)

54″ (135cm) lining
L–XL: 1 yard (0.9m)

54″ (135cm) lining
XS–M: ⅝ yard (0.6m)

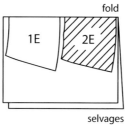

selvages

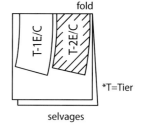

fold

Cutting layout

Assembly

Use a ½" seam allowance unless noted otherwise.

1. Refer to Skirt Basics, Adding the Lining, Steps 1–3 (page 28), to assemble the upper lining first, sewing the darts and the sides together and leaving a 9" opening for the zipper.

2. Sew the contrast lining tier E–C front and back, right sides together, at both side seams. Press the seam allowances open.

3. Pin the upper edge of the lower contrast lining, right side in, to the bottom of the upper lining, wrong side out, matching the side seams. The *right* side of the contrast lining will be facing the *wrong* side of the upper lining. Sew together all around.

4. Open the lining and press the seam allowance up toward the upper lining. On the other side, topstitch just above the contrast lining fabric (sew above the *right* side of the contrast lining fabric).

5. Refer to Skirt Basics again to sew the rest of the skirt together and install the lining the usual way.

6. Refer to Bias Tape Hem (page 41) to make and sew bias tape hems on both the outer skirt and the contrast lining.

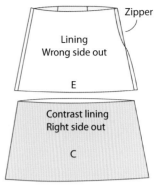

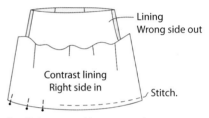

Sew lining top and bottom.

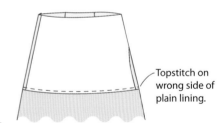

Sew lining top and bottom together.

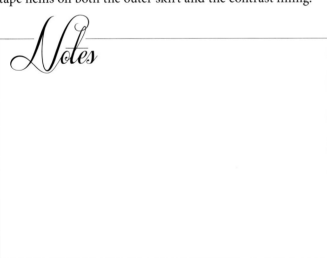

Press seam up and topstitch above lining seam.

Notes

This is such a sweet, breezy skirt.

The side slits and shorter hemline on the outer skirt allow the contrast fabric in the lining to peek out. This is the perfect design for lighter-weight fabrics or rayon.

For this project, I'll show you how to cut the pattern, assemble the contrast lining, and sew the slits in the outer skirt. When that is done, follow the lining instructions (page 28) to complete the skirt.

Cutting

Refer to Tracing Your Pattern (page 19) and the cutting layouts below and on page 70 to trace and cut the desired size of the Skirt Front and Skirt Back patterns.

The usual lining fabric is up at the top (where it can't be seen), and the contrast fabric is at the bottom. Cut the plain lining fabric using the pattern piece cut from the top down to line F. The lower lining is cut from line F down to line A. Be sure to add a ½″ seam allowance at the top of the contrast lining fabric and the bottom of the upper lining fabric.

Cut out the front and back outer pieces the usual way.

OVERSKIRT:
45″–54″ (115–135cm) fabric w/wo nap
XS–XL: 1⅝ yards (1.5m)

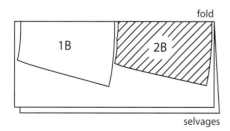

fold

1B   2B

selvages

MASTER PATTERN MARKS

SKIRT LENGTH: Cutting line B

LINING LENGTH: Cutting line for upper lining top to F, contrast lining tier F to A

EXTRA SUPPLIES

FABRIC FOR CONTRAST LINING: 1¼ yards

Layered WITH Side Slit

UPPER LINING:

45″ (115cm) lining
XS: ½ yard (0.5m)

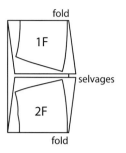

45″ (115cm) lining
S–XL: ¾ yard (0.7m)

54″ (135cm) lining
XL: ¾ yard (0.7m)

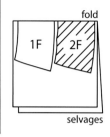

54″ (135cm) lining
XS–L: ½ yard (0.5m)

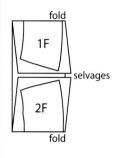

CONTRAST LOWER LINING:

45″–54″ (115–135cm) fabric w/wo nap
XS–XL: 1⅜ yards (1.3m)

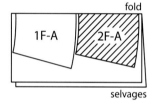

Assembly

Use a ½″ seam allowance unless noted otherwise.

THE LINING

1. Refer to Skirt Basics, Making the Lining (page 28), to sew the darts in the upper lining back and to sew the upper front and upper back lining pieces together along the side seams. Repeat to sew the lower contrast lining front and back pieces together along the side seams. Press the seams open.

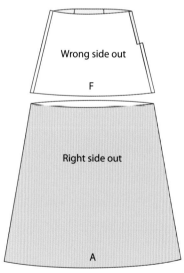

Sew lining sides together.

2. Turn the lower contrast lining right side out. Place the upper lining piece, right side out and upside down, over the lower contrast lining. Match the side seams and pin in place along the F cutting line (the bottom of the upper lining should meet the top of the lower lining).

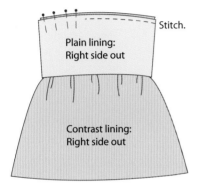

Stitch.

Plain lining:
Right side out

Contrast lining:
Right side out

Sew lining top to lower lining.

3. Press the seam allowance up toward the top and topstitch on the right side of the upper lining fabric. Set the lining aside.

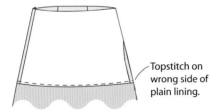

Topstitch on wrong side of plain lining.

Topstitch lining

THE OUTER SKIRT

1. Refer to Skirt Basics (page 24) to sew the darts in the skirt back and install the zipper (page 33). When the zipper is in, don't sew the rest of the seam completely: Stop 11″ down from the top of the skirt. Leave the lower part of the seam open for the lining.

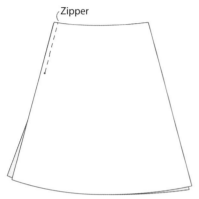

Sew side seam (below zipper) on outer skirt.

2. Sew the other side seam starting at the waist and stopping 11″ down. Snip into the seam allowance just above the end of the stitching line, being careful not to cut into the stitches.

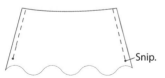

Sew side seam on other side and snip.

3. Finish the seam above the snip using your serger or a zigzag stitch.

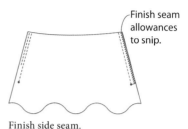

Finish seam allowances to snip.

Finish side seam.

4. Snip into the seam allowance just below the zipper.

5. To finish the skirt slits, make a ¼″ hem on each side (fold over ½″ to wrong side of fabric, press, fold over another ¼″, press).

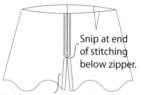

Snip at end of stitching below zipper.

Fold and press opening ½″ back on each side.

Fold under again ¼″.

6. Topstitch around the side slits, sewing up one side and pivoting to sew across the top. Pivot again and sew down the other side.

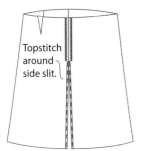

Sew slit hem.

Outside detail of sewn slit hem

7. Refer to Basic ½″ Hem (page 40) to hem both the outer skirt and the lining. Attach the lining to the skirt (page 30). Be sure the *right* side of the upper lining is facing the *right* side of the skirt when you sew them together.

Notes

What a sporty and fun skirt!

You can go for a nautical look by choosing a red or blue fabric and some sharp buttons, or you can mix it up and chose a fun print and whimsical—or even mismatched—buttons. This skirt will look just as great if you choose a longer length for it.

Cutting

Refer to Tracing Your Pattern (page 19) and the cutting layouts below to trace and cut the desired size and length of the Skirt Front and Skirt Back patterns.

Place the Skirt Front pattern piece 3″ away from the fabric fold (parallel to the fold). While cutting the skirt front out, follow the lines at the top and bottom all the way to the fold. Cut the lining in the usual manner.

C LENGTH:

45″–54″ (115–135cm) fabric w/wo nap
XS–XL: 1½ yards (1.4m)

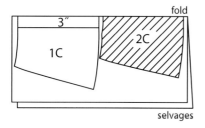

E LENGTH OR LINING:

45″–54″ (115–135cm) fabric w/wo nap
XS–XL: 1 yard (0.9m)

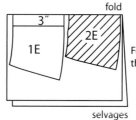

For 1E Lining, don't use the 3″ pleat allowance.

D LENGTH:

45″–54″ (115–135cm) fabric w/wo nap
XS–XL: 1¼ yard (1.1m)

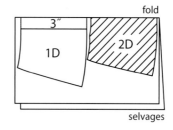

MASTER PATTERN MARKS

SKIRT LENGTH: Between cutting lines C and E

LINING LENGTH: Cutting line E

EXTRA SUPPLIES

6 buttons ⅝″ in diameter

Topstitching thread (*optional*)

Sailor

Assembly

1. Open out the skirt front on your cutting surface and mark the center of the skirt front (you can do this by pressing it while it's still folded if you like).

2. At the waist, measure from the center of the skirt front to the side. Subtract ½" from that number (to compensate for the seam allowance), and then divide this number by 2. Use this number to determine how far from the center you will fold the fabric to make the stitched-down pleats. Mark at this point (on both sides).

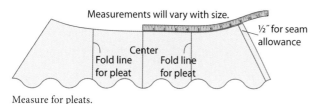

Measure for pleats.

3. Fold at the marks, making sure the folds run parallel to the centerline the whole way down. Press along the fold. Edgestitch the length of the fold (page 37).

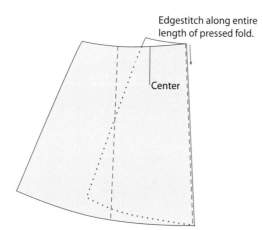

Fold tucks and press.

Edgestitch along folds.

4. Open the skirt to make sure the folds look straight and even.

Finished edgestitched folds

5. Fold again on the edgestitched fold line. To make the stitched-down pleats, sew a 6" line of stitching from the top of the skirt 1" away from the fold line. Repeat on the other side.

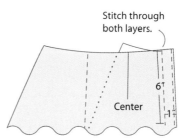

Stitch pleat from top down 6".

6. Press each pleat away from the center of the skirt front.

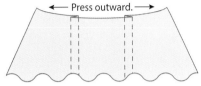

Press pleats away from center.

7. Baste across the top of the skirt, stitching the pleats down, ⅜″ from the top.

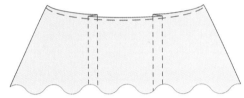

Baste across top edge to secure pleats.

8. Now that the skirt front is done, refer to Skirt Basics (page 27) to sew the rest of the skirt and lining together in the usual fashion. Hem with the basic ½″ hem (page 40).

9. Center 3 buttons on each pleat, placing them 1″, 3″, and 5″ from the finished edge of the waist. Stitch in place (through just the skirt, not the lining).

Sew buttons in marked places.

Inverted pleats made from contrasting fabric add a fun little punch to this flirty skirt. Don't be afraid to use a crazy print for the pleats. While these instructions are for the above-the-knee version, feel free to make this in any length you like. Just make sure you cut the contrast pleat fabric the same length as the skirt.

The front of this skirt is fun to put together, and every pleat has lots of edgestitching to give it shape and hold the crisp fold. The back of the skirt and lining are sewn the usual way, with no changes to the basic assembly.

Cutting

Refer to Tracing Your Pattern (page 19) to trace the Skirt Front pattern and cut it out.

1. Cut the pattern apart on the Contrast Pleat cutting line (3½″ from the fold).

Place the new pattern pieces on the folded fabric, following the cutting diagram below. Make sure to add ½″ to the fabric on either side of the line for the seam allowances. Cut the skirt front and skirt back from the main fabric.

2. Cut 2 rectangles of contrast fabric 8½″ wide and the same length as the skirt front along the fold.

MASTER PATTERN MARKS

SKIRT LENGTH: Cutting line C

LINING LENGTH: Cutting line D

EXTRA SUPPLIES

FABRIC FOR CONTRAST PLEATS:
¼ yard

Topstitching thread (*optional*)

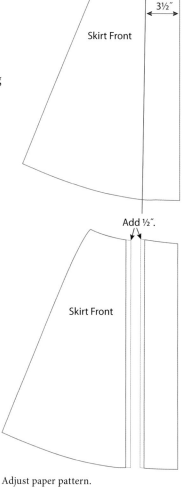

Skirt Front

3½″

Add ½″.

Skirt Front

Adjust paper pattern.

Contrast Pleat

MAIN FABRIC:

45″–54″ (115–135cm) fabric w/wo nap

XS–XL: 1½ yards (1.4m)

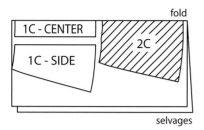

CONTRAST:

45″–54″ (115–135cm) contrast w/wo nap

XS–XL: ¼ yard (0.7m)

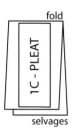

LINING:

45″ (115cm) lining

XS–XL: 1¼ yards (1.1m)

54″ (135cm) lining

M–XL: 1¼ yards (1.1m)

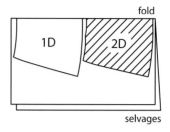

54″ (135cm) lining

XS–S: ¾ yard (0.7m)

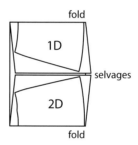

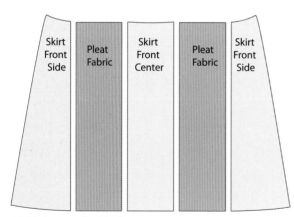

All fabric pieces for skirt front

Assembly

Use a ½" seam allowance unless noted otherwise.

1. Sew a contrast fabric rectangle to either side of the skirt front center piece, matching the long sides.

2. Sew a skirt front side piece to each contrast pleat edge of the skirt front center. Press all the seam allowances toward the skirt fabric. Figure A

3. To make the inverted pleats, fold the skirt over, right sides together, so the pleat is folded on itself. Make sure both seams where the contrast fabric meets the main skirt fabric line up. Pin along the seam. Stitch the pleat together along the main fabric side of the seam, starting at the skirt top and ending 7″ down. Backstitch. Open the skirt front and check to make sure the seam is stitched correctly, with none of the contrast fabric showing through the stitched line. Repeat this process with the other pleat.

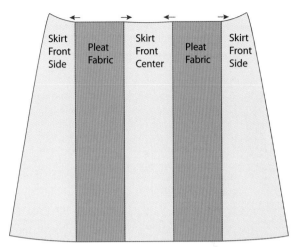

Figure A. Pleat fabric sewn to skirt front pieces. Press toward skirt fabric.

No contrast fabric shows above pleat.

Fold contrast fabric, pin, and stitch pleat alongside seam.

4. On the wrong side of the skirt front, lay the pleat flat, centering the pleat directly over the stitches you just sewed. Press well to crease the folds.

Fold pleat centered on stitching line.

5. Edgestitch all 4 folds on the pleats.

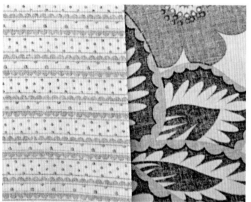

Both pleats edgestitched

6. Turn the skirt right side up. Edgestitch along the fold where the contrast pleat fabric meets the main skirt fabric. Sew up one side of the pleat, pivot, sew across the top of the pleat, pivot again, and sew down the other side.

Edgestitch pleat edges on right side of fabric.

7. Baste across the top of the skirt front, securing the pleats, using a ⅜″ seam allowance.

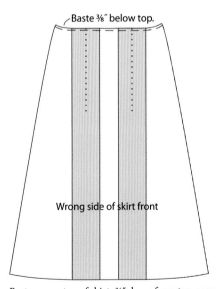

Baste across top of skirt, ⅜″ down from top, securing pleats.

8. Refer to Skirt Basics (page 24) to install the zipper, assemble the skirt and lining, and hem with a basic ½″ hem (page 40).

Notes

This darling skirt with four front pleats and two back pleats has a fun, classic look to it, but you can make it thoroughly modern with some fun fabric. The pleats give this skirt a cute "parochial school" look and add extra movement to it. I've created it here in a flirty mini length. Make it any length and still get beautiful results.

Cutting

Refer to Tracing Your Pattern (page 19) and the cutting layouts on this page to trace and cut the desired size and length of the Skirt Front and Skirt Back pattern pieces.

1. Fold the fabric and place the Skirt Front pattern piece with the "fold edge" of the pattern 4″ away from the fabric fold. Cut the pattern out and just extend the lines at the top and bottom all the way to the fold.

2. Repeat this process with the Skirt Back pattern piece but place the fold edge of the pattern only 1″ from the fabric fold.

MAIN FABRIC:

45″–54″ (115–135cm) fabric w/wo nap

XS–XL: 1¼ yards (1.1m)

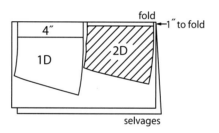

LINING:

45″ (115cm) lining
XS–XL: 1 yard (0.9m)

54″ (135cm) lining
L–XL: 1 yard (0.9m)

54″ (135cm) lining
XS–M: ⅝ yard (0.6m)

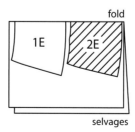

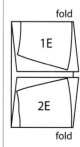

MASTER PATTERN MARKS

SKIRT LENGTH: Cutting line D

LINING LENGTH: Cutting line E

EXTRA SUPPLIES

2″-wide ribbon for sash: 3 yards

Topstitching thread (*optional*)

Double Pleat

Assembly

Use a ½" seam allowance unless noted otherwise.

1. To mark the pleats on the skirt back, place tracing paper between the folded layers of the skirt back. Use the centerline in the darts as your guide (the pleats will replace the darts). Trace the centerline from the top down 3½". Now measure 1" to either side of the center-line and draw a 3½"-long line on each side.

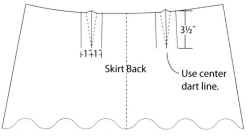

Mark pleats on skirt back.

2. On the skirt front, mark 4 sets of pleat lines (just like the ones on the back of the skirt) using the guide for your skirt size printed on the master pattern.

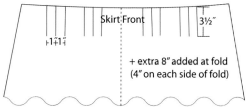

Mark pleats on skirt front.

3. To make a pleat, fold along the center pleat line, right sides together. Match up and pin the outer pleat lines. Pin all the pleats this way.

4. Sew along the marked outer pleat line starting at the top of the skirt piece and sewing down 3½". Backstitch. Repeat to sew all the pleats—2 on Skirt Back and 4 on Skirt Front.

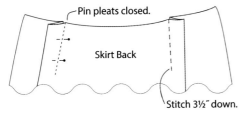

Pin and sew pleats.

5. Press each pleat so the center fold line lies flat against the seam. Baste across the top of the skirt on both the front and back pieces, ⅜" from the edge, securing the pleats.

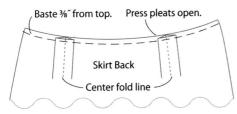

Baste pleats down.

6. Refer to Belt Loops (page 38) to add the optional belt loops to the skirt back.

7. Refer to Skirt Basics (page 24) to assemble the skirt and lining.

8. Finish your skirt with the basic ½" hem (page 40).

Notes

Adorable, sweet, and versatile!

Go crazy with trims and laces on the apron and make this skirt as fun as you can stand. Although I've made it using length D, you can choose any length you like.

Cutting

FABRIC FOR APRON: Cut 1 rectangle according to the desired size below:

Extra-Small: 10″ × 16″

Small: 10″ × 18″

Medium: 10″ × 21″

Large: 10″ × 24″

Extra-Large: 10″ × 27″

FABRIC FOR LINING RUFFLE: Cut the number of strips determined in Step 4 of Ruffled Lining 4½″ × WOF.

Refer to Tracing Your Pattern (page 19) and the cutting layouts on page 90 to trace and cut the desired size and length of the Skirt Front patterns.

To adjust the Skirt Front pattern, use cutting line G for the skirt yoke, and the piece between cutting lines G and D for the lower skirt front. Be sure to add a ½″ seam allowance to the bottom of the yoke piece and the top of the lower skirt piece.

MASTER PATTERN MARKS

SKIRT LENGTH: Cutting line D, between G and D

LINING LENGTH: Cutting line D

EXTRA SUPPLIES

FABRIC FOR APRON: ⅓ yard

FABRIC FOR LINING RUFFLE: ½ yard

Assorted trim, lace, and/or rickrack scraps for apron

Topstitching thread (*optional*)

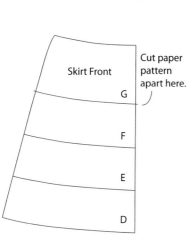

Cut paper pattern.

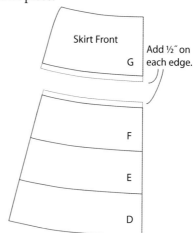

Add ½″ for seam allowances.

Apron Skirt WITH RUFFLE LINING

MAIN FABRIC:

45″ (115cm) fabric w/wo nap
XS–XL: 1⅜ yards (1.3m)

54″ (135cm) fabric w/wo nap
M–XL: 1⅜ yards (1.3m)

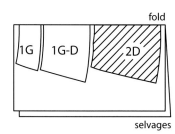

45–54″ (115–135cm) fabric
w/wo nap
XS–S: ¾ yard (0.7m)

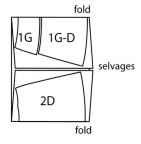

LINING:

45″ (115cm) lining
XS–XL: 1¼ yards (1.1m)

54″ (135cm) lining
M–XL: 1¼ yards (1.1m)

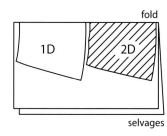

54″ (135cm) lining
XS–S: ¾ yard (0.7m)

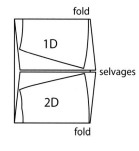

Assembly

Use a ½″ seam allowance unless noted otherwise.

1. On the bottom long edge of the apron piece, sew a ¼″ hem (fold ¼″ to the wrong side of the fabric, press, fold ¼″ again, press, and then topstitch along the upper fold).

2. Add any embellishments to the apron now. Use your imagination and add lace, trim, rickrack, or even an appliqué (page 32).

3. Hem the sides the same way you hemmed the bottom of the apron. Sew 2 rows of gathering stitches across the top of the apron (page 44).

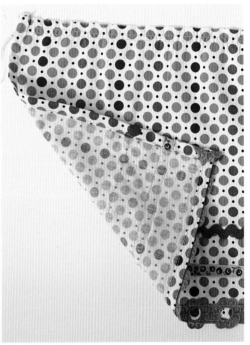

Hem apron sides and gather top.

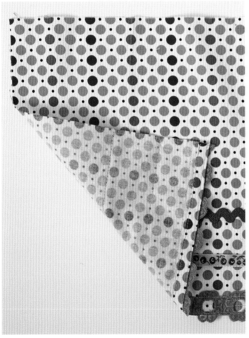

Hem lower edge of apron.

4. Pull the gathering stitches until the top of the apron measures the width listed below for the desired size:

Extra-Small: 9″   Large: 13″

Small: 10″   Extra-Large: 15″

Medium: 11½″

Make sure the gathers are distributed evenly and pin the apron in place, right side up, centered on the top of the lower skirt front, also right side up. Baste across the top of the apron ¼″ from the raw edge.

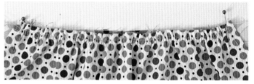

Gather apron and baste to lower skirt.

5. Pin the bottom edge of the yoke to the upper edge of the lower skirt, right sides together (sandwiching the apron in between). Sew the yoke and lower skirt front together.

Pin yoke to lower skirt.

6. Press the seam allowance up toward the yoke. Topstitch above the apron on the right side of the yoke.

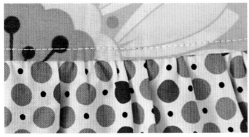

Topstitching on outside of skirt

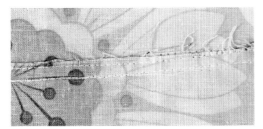

Topstitching on inside of skirt

7. Refer to Skirt Basics (page 24) to complete the skirt (including the zipper installation). Set the skirt aside.

Ruffled Lining

The lining for this skirt is cut at the same length as the skirt because it has a cute ruffle peeking out at the bottom.

1. Refer to Darts (page 25) to sew the darts as directed.

2. Refer to the alternate method (page 29) to sew the lining side seams to ensure that the lining's seam allowances on this short skirt aren't seen.

3. Refer to Making the Lining, Steps 4–6 (page 29), to finish assembling the lining.

4. Refer to Determining the Fabric Length for Ruffles (page 44) and Ruffle Edge Finishes (page 44) to measure the lining hem and make the appropriately sized folded ruffle loop with the 4½″ × WOF ruffle strips.

5. Refer to Gathering Ruffles (page 44) to gather and attach the ruffle hem to the lining. Make sure to pin the ruffle to the wrong side of the lining—the side that faces the skirt fabric (even though the lower edge looks like the right side). Stitch using a ¼″ seam allowance.

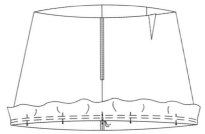

Stitch gathered ruffle to lower lining.

6. Remove the gathering threads and press the seam upward. Topstitch above the ruffle.

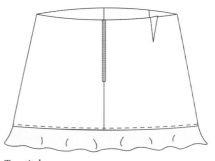

Topstitch.

7. Sew the lining to the skirt (page 30) the usual way. You are done!

I love this skirt!

I've noticed that some designers have been making dresses with solid panels at the sides, giving the illusion that the wearer is much slimmer than she actually is. Brilliant! The eye is naturally drawn to the center of the dress and ignores the solid fabric on the sides. I thought it would be fun to try this with a skirt, and I'm thrilled with the results. I think this design succeeds in taking at least 10 pounds off the wearer—well, off the wearer's appearance anyway! Try it! What have you got to lose?

Cutting

You will be cutting through this pattern, so after you've decided on the skirt length refer to Tracing Your Pattern (page 19) to trace a new pattern from the master pattern.

1. Cut the new Skirt Front and Skirt Back paper pattern pieces along the Take 10 cutting line to make the Skirt Front Center, Skirt Front Side, Skirt Back Center, and Skirt Back Side pattern pieces. Add a ½" seam allowance along the Take 10 cutting line.

MASTER PATTERN MARKS

This skirt uses the Waist Trim pattern piece on the pattern pullout.

SKIRT LENGTH: Cutting line C

LINING LENGTH: Cutting line D

EXTRA SUPPLIES

SOLID FABRIC FOR SIDE PANELS AND WAIST TRIM: ⅜ yard

6 buttons, ¾" to ½" in diameter

Topstitching thread to match solid (*optional*)

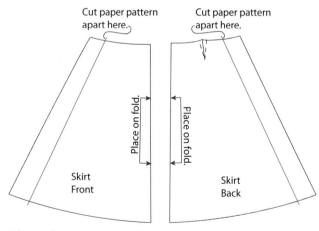

Cut paper pattern apart here.

Cut paper pattern apart here.

Place on fold.

Place on fold.

Skirt Front

Skirt Back

Adjust and cut paper pattern pieces.

Take 10

2. Refer to Tracing Your Pattern (page 19) and the cutting layouts below to cut the skirt front center and skirt back center pieces from the main fabric and the skirt front side and skirt back side pieces from the solid fabric. Figure A

3. Using the Waist Trim pattern on the pattern pullout, cut 6 waist trim pieces from the solid fabric.

A. ½″ seam allowance added

MAIN FABRIC:

45″ (115cm) fabric w/wo nap
XS–S: ⅞ yard (0.8m)

54″ (135cm) fabric w/wo nap
XS–L: ⅞ yard (0.8m)

45″ (115cm) fabric w/wo nap
M–XL: 1½ yards (1.4m)

54″ (135cm) fabric w/wo nap
XL: 1½ yards (1.4m)

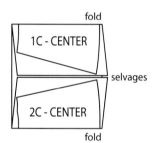

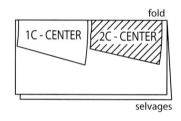

CONTRAST SIDES:

45″–54″ (115–135cm)
fabric w/wo nap
XS–XL: ¾ yard (0.7m)

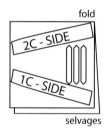

LINING:

45″ (115cm) lining
XS–XL: 1¼ yards (1.1m)

54″ (135cm) lining
M–XL: 1¼ yards (1.1m)

54″ (135cm) lining
XS–S: ¾ yard (0.7m)

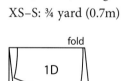

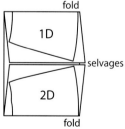

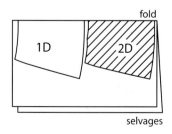

Assembly

Use a ½″ seam allowance unless noted otherwise.

1. Sew the skirt front side pieces to either side of the skirt front center.

2. Repeat Step 1 with the skirt back side pieces and skirt back center.

3. Press the seams toward the center on both skirt pieces.

Skirt front and sides sewn

Skirt back and sides sewn

4. Topstitch along the sides of the center panel next to the seams, catching the seam allowance in the stitching.

Topstitching

Close-up of topstitching on wrong side

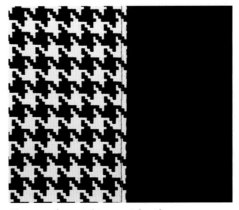

Close-up of topstitching on right side

Adding Waist Trim

1. Place 2 waist trim pieces right sides together. Sew around the edges using a ¼″ seam allowance, leaving a 2″ opening for turning. Trim the corners at an angle to reduce bulk.

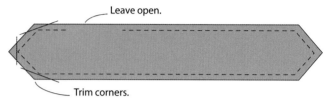

Sewing waist trims

2. Turn right side out and use a chopstick or poking tool to push the corners out. Fold the raw edges inward and press. Edgestitch (page 37) all the way around. Press.

Edgestitched waist trim

3. Repeat Steps 1 and 2 to make 2 more waist trims.

4. Measure 2″ down from the top edge of the skirt. Pin the first waist trim in place, making sure it is centered. Pin the next waist trim 1¼″ down from the bottom of the first. Pin the third an additional 1¼″ down.

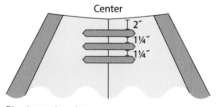

Pinning waist trim

5. Hand sew a button through the center of each pointed end of the waist trims and through the skirt, attaching the waist trims.

Button placement

6. You are now ready to assemble your skirt following the instructions in Skirt Basics (page 24).

Notes

This skirt has a clean, dramatic look

when made with solids. I first envisioned it with bold primary colors, which made me think of traffic signs—hence the name. Feel free to use solids or prints or any combination of the two. You can place folded bias strips or ruffles between the various layers if you really want to have some fun with it.

Cutting

Refer to Tracing Your Pattern (page 19) and the cutting layouts below and on page 102 to trace and cut out the desired size and length of the Skirt Front and Skirt Back patterns. Be sure to add a ½" seam allowance on any of the edges that will be sewn to another skirt piece edge (except for the skirt side seams).

FABRIC 1—BACK & BOTTOM TIER:

45"–54" (115–135cm) fabric w/wo nap
XS–XL: 1 yard (0.9m)

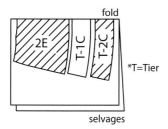

MASTER PATTERN MARKS

SKIRT PIECES: Cut top to E, tier D, tier C

LINING LENGTH: Cutting line D

EXTRA SUPPLIES

FABRIC 1 (BACK AND TIER C): 1 yard

FABRIC 2 (TIER D): ⅜ yard

FABRICS 3 AND 4 (RIGHT AND LEFT SKIRT FRONTS): 1 fat quarter each or ½ yard each

Traffic Stopper

FABRIC 2:

45″–54″ (115–135cm)
fabric w/wo nap
XS–XL: ⅜ yard (0.3m)

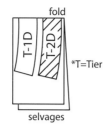

*T=Tier

FABRIC 3:

45″–54″ (115–135cm)
fabric w/wo nap
XS–XL: ½ yard (0.5m)

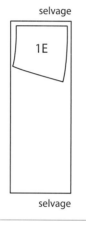

FABRIC 4:

45″–54″ (115–135cm)
fabric w/wo nap
XS–XL: ½ yard (0.5m)

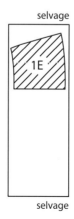

LINING:

45″ (115cm) lining
XS–XL: 1¼ yard (1.1m)

54″ (135cm) lining
M–XL: 1¼ yard (1.1m)

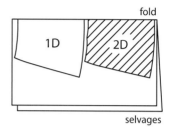

54″ (135cm) lining
XS–S: ¾ yard (0.7m)

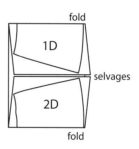

Assembly

1. Refer to Skirt Basics (page 24) to sew the darts in the skirt back.

Sew darts in back.

Skirt Back Fabric 1

E

2. Sew the 2 skirt front pieces together along the center front. Press the center seam allowance to one side and topstitch over the seam allowance on the right side of the fabric.

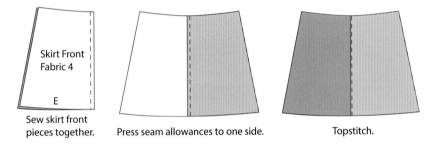

Skirt Front Fabric 4

E

Sew skirt front pieces together.   Press seam allowances to one side.   Topstitch.

3. Sew the tier D front and back pieces, right sides together, at the sides. Press the seam allowances open.

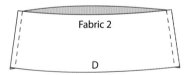

Fabric 2

D

4. Repeat with the Tier C pieces.

Fabric 1

C

5. Install the zipper (page 33) and sew the skirt front and skirt back pieces together.

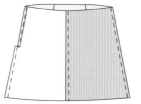

Sew front to back.

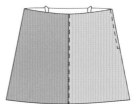

Assembled top section of skirt

6. Pin the top of tier D to the bottom of the skirt, matching the side seams, and sew together using a ½″ seam allowance. Press the seam allowance upward and topstitch above the seam on the right side.

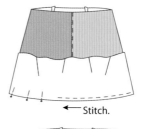

← Stitch.

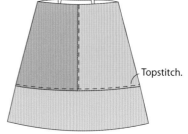

Topstitch.

Sew first tier.

7. Repeat Step 6 with tier C.

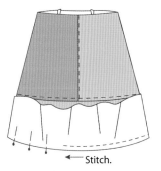

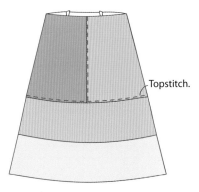

Sew second tier.

8. Your skirt is now ready for you to add the lining (page 28) and finish with a basic ½″ hem (page 40).

Mix and match a variety of fabrics

to make this spunky skirt look different each time. Feel free to use your imagination and try other types of fabric for the pockets, like hankies, or repurposed fabric from clothes you no longer wear. It has a clean, retro feel that you can make your own.

You can use commercial ½″ double-fold bias tape for the pocket trim or quickly make bias tape out of the fabric of your choice (page 41).

In this chapter, I'll show you how to cut the pattern, add the pockets, and finish the front of the skirt. When the skirt front is complete, the rest of the assembly will follow Skirt Basics (page 24).

MASTER PATTERN MARKS

This skirt uses the Pocket pattern on the pattern pullout.

SKIRT LENGTH: Cutting line C

LINING LENGTH: Cutting line D

EXTRA SUPPLIES

FABRIC FOR POCKETS: ⅜ yard

48″ double-fold bias tape

Cutting

Refer to Tracing Your Pattern (page 19) to either trace new patterns or only mark the required pattern sections on your fabric.

Cut the Skirt Front paper pattern apart on cutting line G. The upper section will become the skirt yoke, and the remaining piece will be the lower skirt front. Add ½″ for the seam allowance to the bottom of the yoke and the top of the lower skirt front. Refer to the cutting layout below to cut out the skirt lining fabrics.

MAIN FABRIC:

45″ (115cm) fabric w/wo nap
XS–M: 1⅜ yards (1.3m)

54″ (135cm) fabric w/wo nap
XS–XL: 1⅜ yards (1.3m)

45″ (115cm) fabric w/wo nap
L–XL: 1½ yards (1.4m)

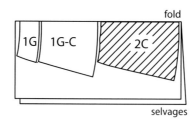

Pocket

CONTRAST POCKETS:

45″– 54″ (115–135cm)
contrast w/wo nap
XS–XL: ⅜ yard (0.4m)

fold

selvages

LINING:

45″ (115cm) lining
XS–XL: 1¼ yards (1.1m)

54″ (135cm) lining
M–XL: 1¼ yards (1.1m)

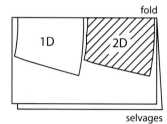
fold

1D   2D

selvages

54″ (135cm) lining
XS–S: ¾ yard (0.7m)

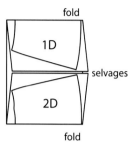
fold

1D

selvages

2D

fold

Making the Pockets

Each pocket is double sided to give it more substance. On my skirt, I used the same fabric for the front of the pocket and the pocket lining. Feel free to use a nice fabric just for the front of the pockets if you don't have enough for the lining. You can use a plain fabric for the lining and nobody will know.

Refer to the cutting layout above to cut 2 pocket fronts and 2 pocket linings on a double layer of fabric. This will yield a pocket and lining that face left, and a pocket and lining that face right.

Cut 2 strips of double-fold bias tape to match the length of the upper pocket edge.

Cut 2 strips of double-fold bias tape to match the length of the lower pocket edge.

1. For each pocket, pin the pocket and lining, wrong sides together, and baste around all sides using a ¼″ seam allowance.

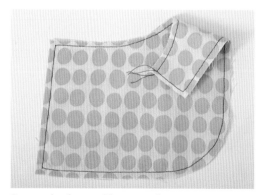

Baste pocket front and lining together.

2. On the back of the pocket (the lining side), pin a length of opened-up double-fold bias tape, right sides together, along the outer edge.

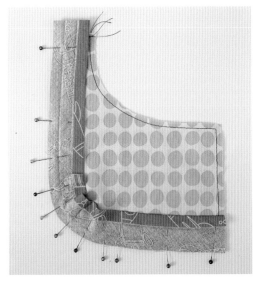

Pin bias to outer pocket.

3. Sew the bias tape to the pocket edge along the fold line (½″ from the edge).

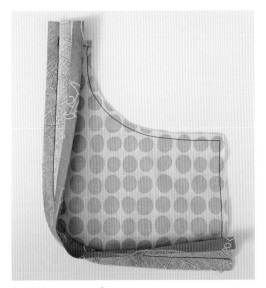

Sew bias to outer pocket.

4. Flip the bias tape over to the right side of the pocket, fold the raw edge under along the fold line, and pin it in place. Make sure the bias tape covers the previous stitching line.

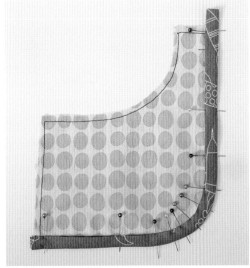

Flip bias over and pin to front.

5. Sew the bias tape in place close to the edge of the fold line. Take your time (especially around the curve) so you get a nice, even stitch.

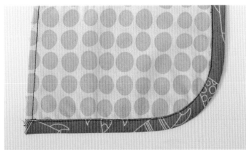

Stitch right side of bias on pocket.

6. Repeat Steps 2–5 with the inner curve of the pocket.

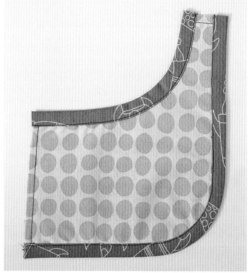

Finish edge on inner curve the same way.

7. Repeat Steps 2–6 with the other pocket.

Assembly

Use a ½″ seam allowance unless noted otherwise.

1. Lay the pockets on the lower skirt front and pin them in place, aligning the pocket at the top and side with the top and side of the skirt piece. Use lots of pins so the pocket doesn't shift. Baste the pockets to the skirt along the top and side edges, ⅜″ from the raw edges.

2. Topstitch along the very lower edge of the pockets, around the outer curves and up to the top, attaching the pockets to the skirt. Again, take your time so you have nice, neat stitching lines.

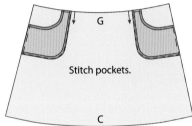

Align and baste at top and sides.

Completed pocket   Completed pocket

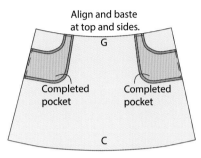

Stitch pockets.

3. Pin the skirt yoke, along its bottom edge, to the upper edge of the lower skirt front, right sides together. Stitch.

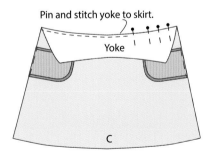

Pin and stitch yoke to skirt.

Yoke

Sew skirt yoke to lower skirt front.

4. On the wrong side, press the seam allowance up toward the yoke. Topstitch on the right side of the skirt front above the seamline.

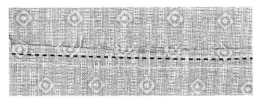

Seam allowance caught in topstitching

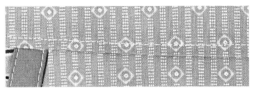

Topstitching on right side of fabric

5. Your skirt front is done! Refer to Skirt Basics (page 24) to finish assembling the skirt. Finish with a basic ½″ hem (page 40).

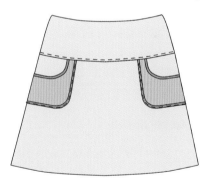

Finished skirt front

$\mathscr{B}$*eautiful and elegant,* this would be a great bridesmaid's skirt for a casual wedding (and you would actually wear it again!). You can use a lace fabric for the overlay or any other sheer fabric. I prefer a simple silky fabric for the underlayer, but feel free to try something else like a cotton print.

Cutting

Refer to Tracing Your Pattern (page 19) and the cutting layouts below to trace and cut the desired size and length of the Skirt Front and Skirt Back patterns in both the underlayer fabric and the lace overlay fabric, as well as the lining fabric.

OVERLAY:

45"–54" (115–135cm) fabric w/wo nap
XS–XL: 1½ yards (1.4m)

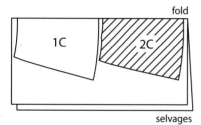

UNDERLAYER FABRIC:

45"–54" (115–135cm) fabric w/wo nap
XS–XL: 1½ yards (1.4m)

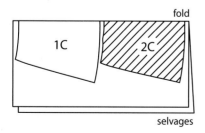

LINING:

45" (115cm) lining
XS–XL: 1¼ yards (1.1m)

54" (135cm) lining
M–XL: 1¼ yards (1.1m)

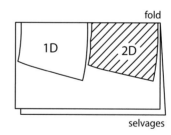

54" (135cm) lining
XS–S: ¾ yard (0.7m)

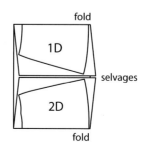

MASTER PATTERN MARKS

SKIRT LENGTH (OVERLAY AND UNDERLAYER): Cutting line C

LINING LENGTH: Cutting line D

EXTRA SUPPLIES

2 yards lace trim

Lace

Assembly

*Use a ½″ seam allowance
unless noted otherwise.*

1. Refer to Skirt Basics (page
24) to sew the darts in both
skirt back pieces.

2. Place the lace overlay
skirt front piece, right side
up, directly on top of the
underlayer skirt front, also
right side up. Pin the lace
overlay and underlayer pieces
together along only the side
seam where the zipper will
be installed. Baste together
10″ down from the top of the
skirt front.

3. Repeat Step 2 with the 2 skirt back pieces.

4. Install the zipper (page 33). Sew only 2″ of the side seam
below the zipper. Snip the seam allowances toward the seam
at the end of your stitching line.

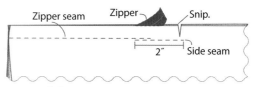

Sew seam below zipper.

5. Fold the lace overlay skirt front and back pieces away
from the underlayer and align at the opposite side seam,
right sides together. Flip the seam allowances out from the
snip below the zipper so the raw edges of the lace are now
facing the opposite direction. Sew the seam all the way
down to the hem. Sew the front and back lace overlay pieces
together along the opposite side seam.

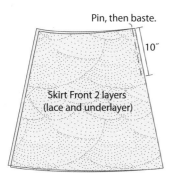

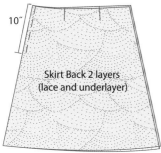

Baste underlayer and overlay together
10″ on side.

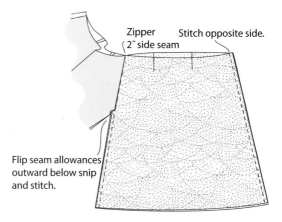

6. Flip the underlayer front and back pieces over so they
cover the lace overlay skirt, right sides together. The underlayer pieces will be wrapped around the lace overlay. Flip out
the underlayer seam allowances below the zipper and continue to sew the side all the way down (make sure the lace
overlay fabric is out of the way). Sew the opposite side seam.

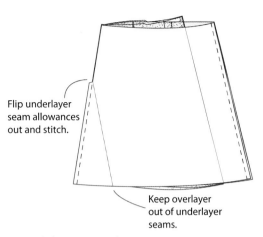

Flip underlayer
seam allowances
out and stitch.

Keep overlayer
out of underlayer
seams.

Sew underlay pieces together.

7. Turn the skirt right side out and baste around the top, ⅜″ down from the top, securing the 2 layers together.

8. Hem the underlayer with a basic ½″ hem (page 40).

9. Sew the coordinating lace trim directly on top of the very bottom of the lace overlay skirt. If the lace fabric has a tendency to fray, use a zigzag stitch. When you reach the ends, tuck them under themselves and stitch.

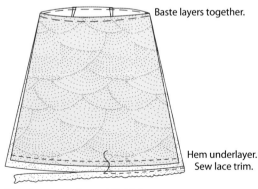

Baste layers together.

Hem underlayer.
Sew lace trim.

Baste layers together and finish hems.

10. Refer to Skirt Basics to make, install, and hem the lining. You're done.

This is the perfect skirt pattern

for using up all those fabric scraps. I've made this one using 5½" squares, but you can use any patchwork design you like. This is also a great way to use a quilt top you might have stuffed in a box somewhere.... Why not wear it?

For this example, I've made a size 6/Small skirt at the C length (above the knee). I made two sets of patchwork fabric panels 7 squares across and 5 squares down. The mini requires only 4 squares down; add another row of squares each time you want to go another tier longer.

Likewise, you will need more squares across for larger sizes (size XL requires 8 rows of squares across instead of 7).

Patchwork Assembly

1. Sew 2 different 5½" × 5½" squares right sides together using a ¼" seam allowance. Press the seam to one side and topstitch on the right side, through the seam allowance.

2. Repeat Step 1 to continue adding squares until you have a row of 7 (or 8) squares.

3. Repeat Steps 1 and 2 to make a total of 5 (or 4 for mini length) patchwork rows.

4. Sew the rows together into a patchwork rectangle. Press and topstitch after each addition.

5. Repeat Steps 1–4 to make a patchwork rectangle for the skirt back.

PATCHWORK CUTTING

Cut the required number of 5½" × 5½" squares as listed below for the desired size and length:

EXTRA-SMALL: 70 (56 for mini length)

SMALL: 70 (56 for mini length)

MEDIUM: 70 (56 for mini length)

LARGE: 70 (56 for mini length)

EXTRA-LARGE: 80 (64 for mini length)

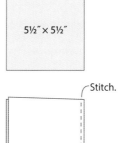

5½" × 5½"

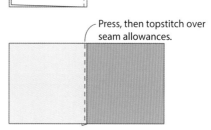

Stitch.

Press, then topstitch over seam allowances.

Sew patches together.

Patchwork

Cutting

1. Fold the patchwork rectangle in half, wrong sides together, along the shorter side, and lay the Skirt Front pattern piece down with the straight edge on the fabric fold. Cut the fabric. Repeat with the Skirt Back pattern piece.

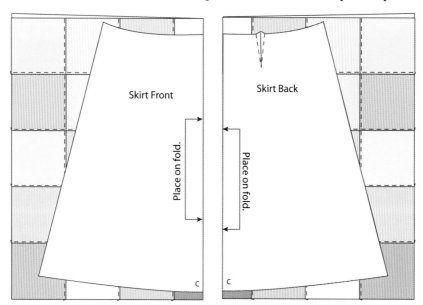

Fold patchwork and lay out pattern pieces.

2. Cut out the lining pieces.

LINING:

45" (115cm) lining
XS–XL: 1¼ yards (1.1m)

54" (135cm) lining
M–XL: 1¼ yards (1.1m)

54" (135cm) lining
XS–S: ¾ yard (0.7m)

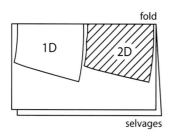

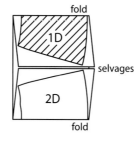

Assembly

Assemble the skirt following Skirt Basics (page 24). Finish with a basic ½" hem (page 40).

Notes

This skirt has a great "hippie chic" look

and is especially nice in soft, flowing fabrics such as linen or rayon. The ruffle is extra wide and has a rolled hem so it doesn't need to be folded over before sewing the gathering stitches.

Cutting

Refer to Tracing Your Pattern (page 19) to cut out the Skirt Front and Skirt Back patterns from the outer fabric and lining.

FABRIC FOR RUFFLE: Cut the number of strips determined in Step 1 of Assembly 4¼″ × WOF.

MAIN FABRIC:

45″–54″ (115–135cm) fabric w/wo nap
XS–XL: 1⅞ yards (1.7m)

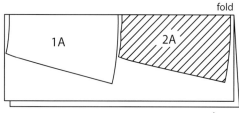

fold

selvages

LINING:

45″–54″ (115–135cm) lining
XS–XL: 1⅝ yards (1.5m)

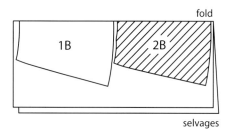

fold

selvages

MASTER PATTERN MARKS

SKIRT LENGTH: Cutting line A

LINING LENGTH: Cutting line B

EXTRA SUPPLIES

FABRIC FOR RUFFLE: ½ yard

Maxi Ruffle

Assembly

Assemble the skirt and lining following Skirt Basics (page 24).

1. After the skirt is assembled, measure the circumference of the hem. Refer to Determining the Fabric Length for Ruffles (page 44) and Ruffle Edge Finishes (page 44) to cut and assemble enough 4¼″ × WOF strips into a rolled-edge ruffle loop to equal that length. You can also finish the ruffle edge by sewing a small zigzag stitch if you want a more "raw" look.

2. Refer to Gathering Ruffles (page 44) to gather the raw edge of the ruffle loop and sew the ruffle to the bottom of the skirt. Press the seam upward and topstitch.

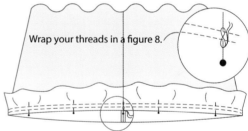

Wrap your threads in a figure 8.

Sew ruffle to maxi skirt.

Notes

Make it

Maternity

MASTER PATTERN MARKS

SKIRT LENGTH: Cutting line C

LINING LENGTH: Cutting line D

EXTRA SUPPLIES

FABRIC FOR MATERNITY PANEL:
⅜ yard stretch knit fabric (I used swimsuit lining for my skirt and loved the stretch in it.)

1 yard ⅜"-wide elastic

Add a stretchy panel to a skirt

and augment your maternity wardrobe. Let the panel out gradually as your waist grows. Then, after the baby comes, tighten it up to have a well-fitting postpartum skirt. And as an added bonus, this skirt requires no zipper!

Cutting

You will be cutting through this pattern, so when you've decided on the skirt length, refer to Tracing Your Pattern (page 19) to trace a new pattern from your master pattern.

Cut your new pattern apart along the Maternity Panel line, adding ½" to the top of the skirt front and the bottom of the maternity panel to allow for the seam allowance when you sew them together. The skirt back and lining back will remain the same.

Refer to the cutting layouts below and on page 125 to cut the adjusted skirt front and lining front, standard skirt back, and two stretch maternity panels.

MAIN FABRIC:

45"–54" (115–135cm) fabric w/wo nap
XS–XL: 1⅜ yards (1.3m)

STRETCH PANEL:

45" (115cm) fabric w/wo nap
XS–XL: ⅜ yard (0.4m)

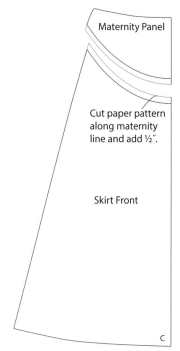

Maternity Panel

Cut paper pattern along maternity line and add ½".

Skirt Front

C

Adjust paper pattern.

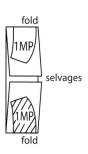

Cutting, continued

LINING:

45″ (115cm) lining
XS–XL: 1⅛ yards (1m)

54″ (135cm) lining
M–XL: 1⅛ yards (1m)

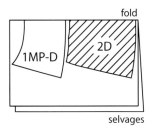

54″ (135cm) lining
XS–S: ¾ yard (0.7m)

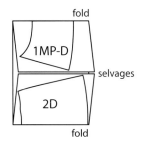

Assembly

Use a ½″ seam allowance unless noted otherwise.

When working with knit fabrics, use a ballpoint needle and
100% polyester thread. I like Coats & Clark All-Purpose or
Dual Duty XP thread.

1. Pin and sew a maternity panel to the skirt front, right
sides together. Figure A

2. Repeat Step 1 with the remaining maternity panel
and the lining front piece. Figure B

3. Refer to Skirt Basics (page 24) to sew the darts in
the skirt back and lining back pieces.

4. Sew the skirt front to the skirt back on the sides (no
zipper needed). Repeat this step with the lining pieces.

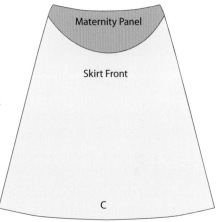

Figure A

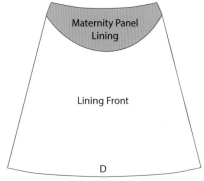

Figure B

5. Finish the side seams by serging or zigzagging.

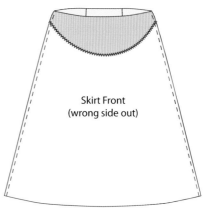

Skirt Front
(wrong side out)

6. Turn the lining right side out and place it inside the skirt, right sides together. Match the side seams and pin well around the top. Stitch the lining and skirt together around the top, using a ½″ seam allowance.

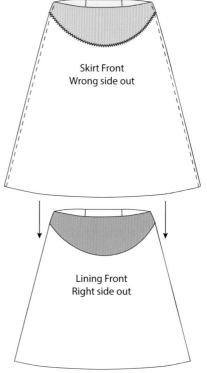

Skirt Front
Wrong side out

Lining Front
Right side out

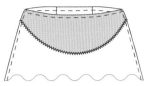

Attach lining to skirt.

7. Turn the skirt right side out and press the seams well. Understitch (sew close to the seamline on the lining through both seam allowances) the lining just on the skirt back.

8. Make a ½″ casing by stitching across the skirt front ½″ down from the finished top edge.

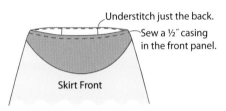

Understitch just the back.

Sew a ½″ casing in the front panel.

Skirt Front

Sew casing into waist.

9. Use a safety pin or bodkin to pull the ⅜″-wide elastic through the casing (you'll have your hand between the skirt and the lining). Sew the end of the elastic in place on one side.

10. Try the skirt on, and pin the elastic in place on the other side after you've adjusted the elastic so the skirt is comfortable. Remove the skirt. Baste securely enough across the other end of elastic so that it holds but so that the stitching is easy to remove as your waist grows. Leave the remaining length of elastic hanging between the skirt and the lining. As adjustments are needed, simply pull the basting stitches and release more elastic into the casing. Then restitch in place.

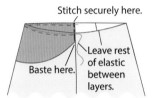

Stitch securely here.

Leave rest of elastic between layers.

Baste here.

Pull elastic through casing.

11. Hem the skirt and lining with a basic ½″ hem (page 40).

12. After you've had your baby, tighten the elastic again so you have a cute and comfortable postpartum skirt.

Notes

Resources

FABRICS

Many of the fabrics pictured in this book came from these wonderful manufacturers:

Andover Fabrics
andoverfabrics.com

Michael Miller Fabrics LLC
michaelmillerfabrics.com

Westminster Fibers
freespiritfabric.com

OTHER SUPPLIES

Dharma Trading Company
dharmatrading.com

Coats & Clark
coatsandclark.com

Clotilde (tracing paper)
clotilde.com

FABRIC SHOPS

Hip Fabric
hipfabric.com

Pink Chalk Fabrics
pinkchalkfabrics.com

Sew, Mama, Sew!
sewmamasew.com

Jona Giammalva shares her love of fabric and her sewing adventures on her blog, Stop Staring and Start Sewing! An avid seamster for more than 25 years, she produces sewing patterns of her original designs under the name Jona G. Pattern Co. When not chasing her five kids or spray painting everything in sight, she can be found in her Arizona home dabbling in her newly acquired quilting hobby.